THE WISI
ABRAHAM LINCOLN

THE WISDOM
OF

Abraham Lincoln

Edited by
Kees de Mooy

CITADEL PRESS
Kensington Publishing Corp.
www.kensingtonbooks.com

CITADEL PRESS BOOKS are published by

Kensington Publishing Corp.
850 Third Avenue
New York, NY 10022

Titles included in the Wisdom Library are published by arrangement with Philosophical Library.

All Kensington titles, imprints, and distributed lines are available at special quantity discounts for bulk purchases for sales promotions, premiums, fund-raising, educational, or institutional use. Special book excerpts or customized printings can be created to fit specific needs. For details, write or phone the office of the Kensington special sales manager: Kensington Publishing Corp., 850 Third Avenue, New York, NY 10022, attn: Special Sales Department; phone 1-800-221-2647.

First Wisdom Library printing: October 2004

10   9   8   7   6   5   4   3   2   1

Printed in the United States of America

Library of Congress Control Number: 2004109739

ISBN 0-8065-2589-4

Contents

Passion has helped us, but can do so no more. It will in future be our enemy. Reason—cold, calculating, unimpassioned reason—must furnish all the materials for our future support and defense. Let those materials be molded into general intelligence, sound morality, and, in particular, a reverence for the Constitution and laws; and that we improved to the last, that we remained free to the last, that we revered his name to the last, that during his long sleep we permitted no hostile foot to pass over or desecrate his resting place, shall be that which to learn the last trump shall awaken our Washington. Upon these let the proud fabric of freedom rest, as the rock of its basis; and as truly as has been said of the only greater institution, "the gates of hell shall not prevail against it."

Abraham Lincoln's Young Men's Lyceum Address (January 27, 1838)

Preface

The Wisdom of Abraham Lincoln consists of extracts from the writings and speeches of the sixteenth president grouped by subject into four major sections: Politics, Civil War, Slavery and Emancipation, and Private Life. As with my previous volumes in the Philosophical Library series—*The Wisdom of John Adams* and *The Wisdom of Thomas Jefferson*—the quotations that I have selected are arranged chronologically, thus giving the reader an opportunity to follow Lincoln's public and private thoughts against the backdrop of current events. Brief introductions help to place the quotes in context. Whereas many collections of quotes pare much of the surrounding material away to expose pithy one-liners, I have endeavored to leave as much of the original selection intact as is necessary to understand Lincoln's full reasoning on the matter at hand. As a further aid to the reader, a timeline with important biographical and historical events has been included.

Timeline of Abraham Lincoln's Life, with Significant Historical Events

1809   **Born in a one-room log cabin near Hodgenville, Kentucky, February 12.**

1816   **Family moved to Indiana.**

1818   **Nancy Hanks Lincoln (mother) died.**

1820   Missouri Compromise

1830   **Family moved to Sangamon River, near Decatur, Illinois.**

1831   **Settled in New Salem, Illinois.**
        Worked as clerk in a small store.
        Made first political speech.
        Nat Turner's slave uprising in Virginia.

1832   **Captain in the Black Hawk War.**
        Defeated for Illinois Legislature.

1833   **Appointed Postmaster of New Salem.**
        Appointed Deputy County Surveyor.
        Britain abolishes slavery.

1834   **Elected to Illinois General Assembly.**
        Began studying law.

1836   **Reelected to a second term in the Illinois General Assembly.**

1836   **Licensed to practice law.**
(*cont.*)   **Began courtship of Mary Owens.**

1837   **Moved from New Salem to Springfield, Illinois.**
             Formed law partnership with John T. Stuart.
             Proposed marriage to Mary Owens but is turned down.

1838   **Delivered Young Men's Lyceum Address.**
             Reelected to a third term in the Illinois General Assembly.

1839   **Practiced law on the 8th Judicial Circuit.**
             Admitted to practice in United States Circuit Court.
             Met Mary Todd.

1840   **Reelected to a fourth term in the Illinois General Assembly.**
             William Henry Harrison is elected president.

1841   **Broken engagement with Mary Todd led to severe bout of depression.**
             Vice President John Tyler becomes president when Harrison dies in office.
             Formed law partnership with Stephen T. Logan.
             Saw slaves chained together on a steamboat trip to Kentucky.

1842   **Almost fought a duel with James Shields.**
             Married Mary Todd November 4.

1843   **Failed to get Whig nomination for U.S. Congress.**
             First son, Robert Todd Lincoln (Bob), born August 1.
1844   **Formed new law partnership with William Herndon.**
             James Polk is elected president.

1845   Texas gains statehood.
             Irish potato famine leads to large increase of immigrants.

1846   Second son, Edward Baker Lincoln (Eddie), born May 1.
           Nominated Whig candidate for U.S. Congress.
           Elected to U.S. House of Representatives.
           Mexican War.

1847   Moves to Washington, D.C., with wife and sons.
           Serves in Congress.

1848   Serves in Congress.
           Campaigns for presidential candidate Zachary Taylor.
           Mexican War ends with U.S. gaining over 500,000
           square miles of territory.
           Zachary Taylor elected president.

1849   Leaves politics to practice law.
           Granted a patent for boat lifting equipment, the only
           president ever to receive a patent.

1850   Second son, Edward Baker Lincoln (Eddie), died.
           Third son, William Wallace Lincoln (Willie), born
           December 21.
           Millard Fillmore becomes president when Taylor dies in
           office.
           Compromise of 1850 is adopted by Congress.

1851   Thomas Lincoln (father) died.

1852   *Uncle Tom's Cabin* is published.
           Franklin Pierce is elected president.

1853   Fourth son, Thomas Lincoln (Tad), born April 4.

1854   Kansas-Nebraska Act threatens Missouri Compromise.
           Elected to Illinois legislature, but declines seat in
           order to run for U.S. Senate.

1855   Lost bid for U.S. Senate.
           Frederick Douglass publishes *My Bondage and My
           Freedom*.

1856   **Became affiliated with the Republican Party.**
            Ran as vice president under John Frémont.
            Massachusetts Senator Charles Sumner is caned by
            South Carolina Senator Preston Brooks.

1857   Dred Scott decision.

1858   **Received Republican nomination for U.S. Senate.**
            Delivered "House Divided" speech.
            Lincoln and Democratic rival Stephen A. Douglas
            met in seven debates.

1859   **Lost U.S. Senate bid to Stephen A. Douglas.**
            John Brown's raid on Harper's Ferry.

1860   **Cooper Union Address.**
            Lincoln-Douglas debates published.
            Received Republican nomination for president.
            Elected 16th President of the United States November 6.
            South Carolina secedes on December 20.

1861   Confederate States of America formed by South Caro-
            lina, Mississippi, Florida, Alabama, Georgia, and Louisiana.
            Inaugurated March 4.
            Civil War starts on April 12 with Confederate bom-
            bardment of Fort Sumter.
            Texas, Arkansas, Tennessee, Virginia, and North Carolina
            join the Confederacy.
            Union army is defeated in first major battle at Bull Run
            (Manassas), Virginia.
            Lincoln appoints General George B. McClellan to
            lead Army of the Potomac.

1862   **Son William Wallace Lincoln (Willie), died at age 12.**
        Union victory at Antietam, Maryland.
        McClellan replaced with General Ambrose E. Burnside
        Union defeat at Fredericksburg, Virginia.
        West Virginia admitted as a state.

1863   **Emancipation Proclamation takes effect January 1.**
        U.S. Colored Troops formed.
        Burnside replaced with General Joseph Hooker.
        Union defeat at the Battle of Chancellorsville, Virginia.
        Hooker replaced with General George G. Meade.
        Union victory at the Battle of Gettysburg.
        Vicksburg captured by General Ulysses S. Grant.
        Met with abolitionist Frederick Douglass.
        Union defeat at Chickamauga, Georgia.
        Delivered the Gettysburg Address.
        Issued Proclamation of Amnesty and Reconstruction.

1864   **General Ulysses S. Grant made general-in-chief of all
        Union armies.**
        Won Republican nomination for second term.
        Atlanta is captured by General Sherman.
        Union victory in the Shenandoah Valley.
        **Defeated Democrat George B. McClellan for second
        presidential term.**

1865   **Thirteenth Amendment passed in Congress.**
        Inaugurated March 4.
        Gen. Robert E. Lee surrenders at Appomattox, Virginia,
        April 9.
        Gave last public speech April 11.
        Shot at Ford's Theatre by John Wilkes Booth on April 14.
        Died on morning of April 15.

PART I

Politics

Political Beliefs

Abraham Lincoln was first and foremost a politician. Handicapped by his humble origins and a meager education, yet blessed with tremendous rhetorical ability and boundless patriotism, Lincoln led the Republican Party to national prominence during the most tumultuous period of American history. His ungainly appearance made a poor first impression, but he won support by his passionate speeches that could go on for three hours or longer. He shot to national prominence in a series of debates with political foe Stephen Douglas. In countless letters to political allies and enemies alike, Lincoln distinguished himself as a tireless proponent for those issues that he held most dearly, which he summed up as "gratitude to our fathers, justice to ourselves, duty to posterity."

July 1832
From Lincoln's reputed first political speech, delivered in Pappsville, Illinois.

I presume you all know who I am. I am humble Abraham Lincoln. I have been solicited by many friends to become a candidate for the Legislature. My politics are short and sweet, like the old woman's dance. I am in favor of a national bank. I am in favor of the internal improvement system, and a high protective tariff. These are my sentiments and political principles. If elected, I shall be thankful; if not it will all be the same.

(NH XI, 97)

June 13, 1836
A letter to the editor of the Sangamo Journal, *written during Lincoln's campaign for a second term in the Illinois legislature.*

I go for all sharing the privileges of the government, who assist in bearing its burthens. Consequently I go for admitting all whites to the right of suffrage who pay taxes or bear arms (by no means excluding females).

If elected, I shall consider the whole people of Sangamon my constituents, as well those that oppose, as those that support me.

While acting as their representative, I shall be governed by their will, on all subjects upon which I have the means of knowing what their will is; and upon all others, I shall do what my own judgment teaches me will best advance their interests. Whether elected or not, I go for distributing the proceeds of the sales of the public lands to the several states, to enable our state, in common with others, to dig canals and construct railroads, without borrowing money and paying interest on it.

(CW I, 48)

January 27, 1838
Young Men's Lyceum speech, delivered in Springfield, Illinois. (See Appendix A for complete text)

In the great journal of things happening under the sun, we, the American people, find . . . ourselves in the peaceful possession of the fairest portion of the earth as regards extent of territory, fertility of soil, and salubrity of climate. We find ourselves under the government of a system of political institutions conducing more essentially to the ends of civil and religious liberty than any of which the history of former times tells us. We, when mounting the stage of existence, found ourselves the legal inheritors of these fundamental blessings. We toiled not in the acquirement or establishment of them; they are a legacy bequeathed us by a once hardy, brave, and patriotic, but now lamented and departed, race of ancestors. Theirs was the task (and nobly they performed it) to possess themselves, and through themselves us, of this goodly land,

and to uprear upon its hills and its valleys a political edifice of liberty and equal rights; 'tis ours only to transmit these—the former unprofaned by the foot of an invader, the latter undecayed by the lapse of time and untorn by usurpation—to the latest generation that fate shall permit the world to know. This task of gratitude to our fathers, justice to ourselves, duty to posterity, and love for our species in general, all imperatively require us faithfully to perform.

(NH I, 35–36)

January 27, 1838
Young Men's Lyceum speech.

Let every American, every lover of liberty, every well-wisher to his posterity swear by the blood of the Revolution never to violate in the least particular the laws of the country, and never to tolerate their violation by others. As the patriots of '76 did to the support of the Declaration of Independence, so to the support of the Constitution and laws let every American pledge his life, his property, and his sacred honor—let every man remember that to violate the law is to trample on the blood of his father, and to tear the charter of his own and his children's liberty. Let reverence for the laws be breathed by every American mother to the lisping babe that prattles on her lap; let it be taught in schools, in seminaries, and in colleges; let it be written in primers, spelling-books, and in almanacs; let it be preached from the pulpit, proclaimed in legislative halls, and enforced in courts of justice. And, in short, let it become the political religion of the nation; and let the old and the young, the rich and the poor, the grave and the gay of all sexes and tongues and colors and conditions, sacrifice unceasingly upon its altars.

(NH I, 42–43)

January 27, 1838
Young Men's Lyceum speech.

Reason—cold, calculating, unimpassioned reason—must furnish all the materials for our future support and defense. Let those materials be molded into general intelligence, sound morality, and, in particular, a reverence for the Constitution and laws; and that we improved to the last, that we remained free to the last, that we revered his name to the last, that during his long sleep we permitted no hostile foot to pass over or desecrate his resting place, shall be that which to learn the last trump shall awaken our Washington.

(NH I, 50)

January 28, 1838
From the Young Men's Lyceum Address, Lincoln's view on the current danger to American government.

That our government should have been maintained in its original form, from its establishment until now, is not much to be wondered at. It had many props to support it through that period, which now are decayed and crumbled away. Through that period it was felt by all to be an undecided experiment; now it is understood to be a successful one. Then, all that sought celebrity and fame and distinction expected to find them in the success of that experiment. Their all was staked upon it; their destiny was inseparably linked with it. Their ambition aspired to display before an admiring world a practical demonstration of the truth of a proposition which had hitherto been considered at best no better than problematical—namely, the capability of a people to govern themselves. If they succeeded they were to be immortalized; their names were to be transferred to counties, and cities, and rivers, and mountains; and to be revered and sung, toasted through all time. If they failed, they were to be called knaves, and fools, and fanatics for a fleeting hour; then to sink and be forgotten. They succeeded. The experiment is successful, and thousands have won their deathless names in making it so. But the game is caught; and I believe it is true that with the catching end the pleasures of the chase.

(NH I, 45–46)

December 20, 1839
From a speech in the Illinois House of Representatives.

Many countries have lost their liberty, and ours may lose hers; but if she shall, be it my proudest plume, not that I was the last to desert, but that I never deserted her.

(NH I, 137)

December 20, 1839
From a speech in the Illinois House of Representatives.

If ever I feel the soul within me elevate and expand to those dimensions not wholly unworthy of its almighty Architect, it is when I contemplate the cause of my country, deserted by all the world beside, and I standing up boldly and alone, and hurling defiance at her victorious oppressors. Here, without contemplating consequences, before high heaven and in the face of the world, I swear eternal fidelity to the just cause, as I deem it, of the land of my life, my liberty, and my love.

(NH I, 138)

February 22, 1842
Comment to a friend regarding a speech he had just delivered to a temperance society on the anniversary of George Washington's birth.

I have just told the folks here in Springfield on this 110th anniversary of the birth of him whose name, mightiest in the cause of civil liberty, still mightiest in the cause of moral reformation, we mention in solemn awe, in naked, deathless splendor, that the one victory we can claim is that there is not one slave or one drunkard on the face of God's green earth.

(NH I, 191–92)

February 15, 1845
Lincoln's opinion on Executive's right to declare war without the consent of Congress.

The provision of the Constitution giving war-making power to Congress was dictated, as I understand it, by the following reasons. Kings had always been involving and impoverishing their people in wars, pretending generally, if not always, that the good of the people was the object. This our convention understood to be the most oppressive of all kingly oppressions; and they resolved to so frame the Constitution that no one man should hold the power of bringing this oppression upon us. But your view destroys the whole matter, and places our president where kings have always stood.

(CW I, 451–52)

December 1, 1847
During a tariff discussion, prior to taking his seat in Congress.

It seems to be an opinion very generally entertained that the condition of a nation is best whenever it can buy cheapest; but this is not necessarily true, because if at the same time and by the same cause, it is compelled to sell correspondingly cheap, nothing is gained. Then it is said the best condition is when we can buy cheapest and sell dearest; but this again is not necessarily true, because with both these we might have scarcely anything to sell, or, which is the same thing, to buy with.

(NH I, 304)

January 12, 1848
Lincoln argued that President James K. Polk's invasion and seizure of lands in the Mexican War was unconstitutional.

When the war began, it was my opinion that all those who, because of knowing too little, or because of knowing too much, could not conscientiously approve the conduct of the president, in the beginning of it, should, nevertheless, as good citizens and patriots, remain silent on that point, at least till the war should be ended. . . . I carefully examined the president's messages, to ascertain what he himself had said and proved upon the point. The result of this examination was to make the impression, that taking for true, all the president states as facts, he falls far short of proving his justification; and that the president would have gone farther with his proof, if it had not been for the small matter, that the truth would not permit him. . . .

His mind, tasked beyond its power, is running hither and thither, like some tortured creature, on a burning surface, finding no position, on which it can settle down, and be at ease. . . . As I have said before, he knows not where he is. He is a bewildered, confounded, and miserably perplexed man. God grant he may be able to show, there is not something about his conscience, more painful than all his mental perplexity!

(CW I, 432–42)

February 13, 1848
Lincoln on the Electoral College.

I was once of your opinion, expressed in your letter, that presidential electors should be dispensed with, but a more thorough knowledge of the causes that first introduced them has made me doubt. The causes were briefly these. The convention that framed the Constitution had this difficulty: that small states wished to so form the new government as that they might be equal to the large ones, regardless of the inequality of population; the large ones insisted on equality in proportion to population. They compromised it by basing the House of Representatives on population, and the Senate on states regardless of population, and the execution of both principles by electors in each state, equal in number to her Senators and Representatives.

(NH I, 356)

February 15, 1848
Opinion on the constitutionality of President Polk's seizure of territory during the Mexican War.

That soil was not ours; and Congress did not annex or attempt to annex it. . . . Allow the president to invade a neighboring nation, whenever he shall deem it necessary to repel an invasion, and you allow him to do so, whenever he may choose to say he deems it necessary for such purpose—and you allow him to make war at pleasure. Study to see if you can fix any limit to his power in this respect, after you have given him so much as you propose. If, today, he should choose to say he thinks it necessary to invade Canada, to prevent the British from invading us, how could you stop him? You may say to him, "I see no probability of the British invading us" but he will say to you "be silent; I see it, if you don't."

(CW I, 451)

June 20, 1848
From a speech in the House of Representatives.

The true rule in determining to embrace or reject anything, is not whether it have any evil in it; but whether it have more of evil, than of good. There are few things wholly evil, or wholly good. Almost everything, especially of governmental policy, is an inseparable compound of the two; so that our best judgment of the preponderance between them is continually demanded.

(CW I, 484)

June 20, 1848
Lincoln's opinion on Constitutional amendments.

As a general rule, I think we would much better let it alone. No slight occasion should tempt us to touch it. Better not take the first step, which may lead to a habit of altering it. Better, rather, habituate ourselves to think of it as unalterable. It can scarcely be made better than it is. New provisions would introduce new difficulties, and thus create and increase appetite for further change.

No sir, let it stand as it is. New hands have never touched it. The men who made it have done their work, and have passed away. Who shall improve on what they did?

(CW I, 488)

July 25, 1850
From a eulogy for President Zachary Taylor.

I will not pretend to believe that all the wisdom, or all the patriotism of the country, died with General Taylor. But we know that wisdom and patriotism, in a public office, under institutions like ours, are wholly inefficient and worthless, unless they are sustained by the confidence and devotion of the people.

(CW II, 89)

July 16, 1852
Introduction to a eulogy for Henry Clay, delivered at the State House in Springfield, Illinois. Clay was the author of the Missouri Compromise and was a major influence on Lincoln's political outlook.

On the fourth day of July, 1776, the people of a few feeble and oppressed colonies of Great Britain, inhabiting a portion of the Atlantic coast of North America, publicly declared their national independence, and made their appeal to the justice of their cause and to the God of battles for the maintenance of that declaration. That people were few in number and without resources, save only their wise heads and stout hearts. Within the first year of that declared independence, and while its maintenance was yet problematical—while the bloody struggle between those resolute rebels and their haughty would-be masters was still waging—of undistinguished parents and in an obscure district of one of those colonies Henry Clay was born. The infant nation and the infant child began the race of life together. For three quarters of a century they have traveled hand in hand. They have been companions ever. The nation has passed its perils, and it is free, prosperous, and powerful. The child has reached his manhood, his middle age, his old age, and is dead. In all that has concerned the nation the man ever sympathized; and now the nation mourns the man.

(NH II, 155–56)

July 16, 1852
From the eulogy for Henry Clay.

It is probably true he owed his preeminence to no one quality, but to a fortunate combination of several. He was surpassingly eloquent; but many eloquent men fail utterly, and they are not, as a class, generally successful. His judgment was excellent; but many men of good judgment live and die unnoticed. His will was indomitable; but this quality often secures to its owner nothing better than a character for useless obstinacy. These, then, were Mr. Clay's leading qualities. No one of them is very uncommon; but all together are rarely combined in a single individual, and this is probably the reason why such men as Henry Clay are so rare in the world. . . .

Mr. Clay's predominant sentiment, from first to last, was a deep devotion to the cause of human liberty—a strong sympathy with the oppressed everywhere, and an ardent wish for their elevation. With him this was a primary and all-controlling passion. Subsidiary to this was the conduct of his whole life. He loved his country partly because it was his own country, and mostly because it was a free country; and he burned with a zeal for its advancement, prosperity, and glory, because he saw in such the advancement, prosperity, and glory of human liberty, human right, and human nature. He desired the prosperity of his countrymen, but chiefly to show to the world that free men could be prosperous.

(NH II, 163–65)

July 1, 1854
Part of a fragment on government.

Government is a combination of the people of a country to effect certain objects by joint effort. The best framed and best administered governments are necessarily expensive; while by errors in frame and maladministration most of them are more onerous than they need be, and some of them very oppressive.

(NH II, 182)

July 1, 1854
Another fragment on government.

In all that the people can individually do as well for themselves, government ought not to interfere.

(NH II, 187)

February 28, 1857
The Republican Party political platform was opposed to the expansion of slavery.

Upon those men who are, in sentiment, opposed to the spread, and nationalization of slavery, rests the task of preventing it. The Republican organization is the embodiment of that sentiment; though, as yet, it by no means embraces all the individuals holding that sentiment. . . . And yet, a year ago, they stood up, an army over thirteen thousand strong. That army is, today, the best hope of the nation, and of the world. Their work is before them; and from which they may not guiltless turn away.

(CW II, 391)

May 18, 1858
Notes for a speech on the Lecompton Constitution, a controversial document that would allow slavery in the Kansas Territory, which was applying for statehood.

I am for the people of the whole nation doing just as they please in all matters which concern the whole nation; for those of each part doing just as they choose in all matters which concern no other part; and for each individual doing just as he chooses in all matters which concern nobody else.

(CW II, 452)

July 10, 1858
During a debate with Stephen A. Douglas in Chicago, Lincoln reiterated his support for states' rights.

I think that I have said it in your hearing—that I believe each individual is naturally entitled to do as he pleases with himself and the fruit of his labor, so far as it in no wise interferes with any other man's rights; that each community, as a state, has a right to do exactly as it pleases with all the concerns within that state that interfere with the right of no other state; and that the general government, upon principle, has no right to interfere with anything other than that general class of things that does not concern the whole.

(NH III, 35–36)

July 10, 1858
During a speech in Chicago, Lincoln explained the connection that immigrants could make with the rights embodied in the Declaration of Independence.

If they look back through this history to trace their connection with those days by blood, they find they have none; they cannot carry themselves back into that glorious epoch and make themselves feel that they are a part of us; but when they look through that old Declaration of Independence, they find that those old men say that "We hold these truths to be self-evident, that all men are created equal," and then they feel that the moral sentiment taught in that day evidences their relation to those men, that it is the father of all moral principle in them, and that they have a right to claim it as though they were blood of the blood, and flesh of the flesh, of the men who wrote that Declaration, and so they are. That is the electric cord in that Declaration that links the hearts of patriotic and liberty-loving men together, that will link those patriotic hearts as long as the love of freedom exists in the minds of men throughout the world.

(NH III, 47–48)

August 21, 1858
Part of Lincoln's reply to Stephen A. Douglas during their first debate.

In this and like communities, public sentiment is everything. With public sentiment, nothing can fail; without it, nothing can succeed. Consequently he who molds public sentiment goes deeper than he who enacts statutes or pronounces decisions.

(NH III, 252)

October 1, 1858
From notes Lincoln made for his debates with Stephen Douglas.

Allow me, in my own way, to state with what aims and objects I did enter upon this campaign. I claim no extraordinary exemption from personal ambition. That I like preferment as well as the average of men may be admitted. But I protest I have not entered upon this hard contest solely, or even chiefly, for a mere personal object. I clearly see, as I think, a powerful plot to make slavery universal and perpetual in this nation. The effort to carry that plot through will be persistent and long continued, extending far beyond the senatorial term for which Judge Douglas and I are just now struggling. I enter upon the contest to contribute my humble and temporary mite in opposition to that effort.

(NH IV, 214)

February 22, 1859
From a speech on discoveries and inventions.

The human family originated, as is thought, somewhere in Asia, and have worked their way principally westward. Just now in civilization and the arts the people of Asia are entirely behind those of Europe; those of the east of Europe are behind those of the west of it; while we, here, in America, think we discover, and invent, and improve faster than any of them. They may think this is arrogance; but they cannot deny that Russia has called on us to show her how to build steamboats and railroads, while in the older parts of Asia they scarcely know that such things as steamboats and railroads exist. In anciently inhabited countries, the dust of ages . . . seems to settle upon and smother the intellects and energies of man. It is in this view that I have mentioned the discovery of America as an event greatly favoring and facilitating useful discoveries and inventions.

(NH V, 112–13)

April 6, 1859
An explanation of the difference between Democrats and Republicans prior to the Civil War.

Bearing in mind that about seventy years ago, two great political parties were first formed in this country, that Thomas Jefferson as the head of one of them, and Boston the headquarters of the other, it is both curious and interesting that those supposed to descend politically from the party opposed to Jefferson, should now be celebrating his birthday in their own original seat of empire, while those claiming political descent from him have nearly ceased to breathe his name everywhere.

Remembering too, that the Jefferson party were formed upon their supposed superior devotion to the personal rights of men, holding their rights of property to be secondary only, and greatly inferior, and then assuming that the so-called democracy of today, are the Jefferson, and their opponents, the anti-Jefferson parties, it will be equally interesting to note how completely the two have changed hands as to the principle upon which they were originally supposed to be divided.

The democracy of today hold the liberty of one man to be absolutely nothing, when in conflict with another man's right of property. Republicans, on the contrary, are for both the man and the dollar; but in cases of conflict, the man before the dollar.

(CW III, 374–75)

February 22, 1860
From a lecture to the Springfield Library Association, in which
Lincoln described Stephen Douglas's supporters, who supported
the younger Douglas over older politicians such as Buchanan.

We have all heard of Young America. He is the most current youth of the age. Some think him conceited and arrogant; but has he not reason to entertain a rather extensive opinion of himself? Is he not the inventor and owner of the present, and sole hope of the future? Men and things, everywhere, are ministering unto him . . . He owns a large part of the world, by right of possessing it, and all the rest by right of wanting it, and intending to have it. . . . He is a great friend of humanity; and his desire for land is not selfish, but merely an impulse to extend the area of freedom. . . . His horror is for all that is old, particularly "Old Fogy"; and if there be anything old which he can endure, it is only old whisky and old tobacco.

(NH V, 99–100)

February 27, 1860
From an address at the Cooper Institute, New York.

What is the frame of government under which we live? The answer must be, "The Constitution of the United States." That Constitution consists of the original framed in 1787, and under which the present government first went into operation, and twelve subsequently framed amendments, the first ten of which were framed in 1789.

(NH V, 294)

February 27, 1860
Address at the Cooper Institute.

I do not mean to say we are bound to follow implicitly in whatever our fathers did. To do so would be to discard all the lights of current experience—to reject all progress, all improvement. What I do say is that if we would supplant the opinions and policy of our fathers in any case, we should do so upon evidence so conclusive, and argument so clear, that even their great authority, fairly considered and weighed, cannot stand; and most surely not in a case whereof we ourselves declare they understood the question better than we.

(NH V, 308)

March 6, 1860
From a speech in Hartford, Connecticut.

I don't believe in a law to prevent a man from getting rich; it would do more harm than good. So while we do not propose any war upon capital, we do wish to allow the humblest man an equal chance to get rich with everybody else. When one starts poor, as most do in the race of life, free society is such that he knows he can better his condition; he knows that there is no fixed condition of labor for his whole life.

(NH V, 361)

February 12, 1861
Lincoln's stand on immigration, from a speech in Cincinnati prior to his inauguration.

In regard to Germans and foreigners, I esteem them no better than other people, nor any worse. It is not my nature, when I see a people borne down by the weight of their shackles—the oppression of tyranny—to make their life more bitter by heaping upon them greater burdens; but rather would I do all in my power to raise the yoke than to add anything that would tend to crush them.

Inasmuch as our country is extensive and new, and the countries of Europe are densely populated, if there are any abroad who desire to make this the land of their adoption, it is not in my heart to throw aught in their way to prevent them from coming to the United States.

(NH VI, 120–21)

February 21, 1861
*In an address to the New Jersey Senate shortly after he was elected
president, Lincoln cited one of his early influences.*

May I be pardoned if, upon this occasion, I mention that away
back in my childhood, the earliest days of my being able to read, I
got hold of a small book, such a one as few of the younger members have ever seen—Weems' "Life of Washington." I remember
all the accounts there given of the battlefields and struggles for the
liberties of the country, and none fixed themselves upon my imag-
ination so deeply as the struggle here at Trenton, New Jersey. The
crossing of the river, the contest with the Hessians, the great
hardships endured at that time, all fixed themselves on my memory more than any single Revolutionary event; and you all know,
for you have all been boys, how these early impressions last longer
than any others. I recollect thinking then, boy even though I was,
that there must have been something more than common that
these men struggled for. I am exceedingly anxious that that
thing—that something even more than national independence;
that something that held out a great promise to all the people of
the world to all time to come—I am exceedingly anxious that this
Union, the Constitution, and the liberties of the people shall be
perpetuated in accordance with the original idea for which that
struggle was made, and I shall be most happy indeed if I shall be a
humble instrument in the hands of the Almighty and of this, his
almost chosen people, for perpetuating the object of that great
struggle.

(NH VI, 151)

February 22, 1861
From an address at Independence Hall, Philadelphia.

I have often pondered over the dangers which were incurred by
the men who assembled here and framed and adopted that
Declaration. I have pondered over the toils that were endured by
the officers and soldiers of the army who achieved that indepen-

dence. I have often inquired of myself what great principle or idea it was that kept this Confederacy so long together. It was not the mere matter of separation of the colonies from the motherland, but that sentiment in the Declaration of Independence which gave liberty not alone to the people of this country, but hope to all the world, for all future time. It was that which gave promise that in due time the weights would be lifted from the shoulders of all men, and that all should have an equal chance. This is the sentiment embodied in the Declaration of Independence.

(NH VI, 157)

February 22, 1861
From an address at Independence Hall, Philadelphia.

I have said nothing but what I am willing to live by, and, if it be the pleasure of Almighty God, to die by.

(NH VI, 158)

March 4, 1861
From Lincoln's first inaugural address. (See Appendix C for complete text.)

Physically speaking, we cannot separate. We cannot remove our respective sections from each other, nor build an impassable wall between them. A husband and wife may be divorced, and go out of the presence and beyond the reach of each other; but the different parts of our country cannot do this. They cannot but remain face to face, and intercourse, either amicable or hostile, must continue between them. Is it possible, then, to make that intercourse more advantageous or more satisfactory after separation than before? Can aliens make treaties easier than friends can make laws? Suppose you go to war, you cannot fight always; and when, after much loss on both sides, and no gain either, you cease fighting, the identical old questions as to terms of intercourse are again upon you.

(NH VI, 181–82)

March 4, 1861
From Lincoln's first inaugural address.

I hold that, in contemplation of universal law and of the Constitution, the Union of these states is perpetual. Perpetuity is implied, if not expressed, in the fundamental law of all national governments. It is safe to assert that no government proper ever had a provision in its organic law for its own termination.

(NH VI, 173)

March 4, 1861
From Lincoln's first inaugural address.

This country, with its institutions, belongs to the people who inhabit it.

(NH VI, 182)

July 4, 1861
From a special session of government, convened at the beginning of the Civil War.

Our popular government has often been called an experiment. Two points in it our people have already settled—the successful establishing and the successful administering of it. One still remains—its successful maintenance against a formidable internal attempt to overthrow it. It is now for them to demonstrate to the world that those who can fairly carry an election can also suppress a rebellion; that ballots are rightful and peaceful successors of bullets; and that when ballots have fairly and constitutionally decided, there can be no successful appeal back to bullets; that there can be no successful appeal, except to ballots themselves, at succeeding elections. Such will be a great lesson of peace: teaching men that what they cannot take by an election, neither can they take it by a war; teaching all the folly of being the beginners of a war.

(NH VI, 322)

December 3, 1861
From the annual message to Congress.

Since the organization of the government, Congress has enacted some 5,000 acts and joint resolutions, which fill more than 6,000 closely printed pages, and are scattered through many volumes. Many of these acts have been drawn in haste and without sufficient caution, so that their provisions are often obscure in themselves, or in conflict with each other, or at least so doubtful as to render it very difficult for even the best informed persons to ascertain precisely what the statute law really is.

(NH VII, 40)

December 3, 1861
From the annual message to Congress.

No men living are more worthy to be trusted than those who toil up from poverty—none less inclined to take or touch aught which they have not honestly earned.

(NH VII, 59)

July 7, 1863
Response to a group of well-wishers at the White House, during a celebration of the Union victory at Vicksburg.

I am very glad indeed to see you tonight, and yet I will not say I thank you for this call; but I do most sincerely thank Almighty God for the occasion on which you have called. How long ago is it? Eighty-odd years since, on the Fourth of July, for the first time in the history of the world, a nation, by its representatives, assembled and declared, as a self-evident truth, "that all men are created equal." That was the birthday of the United States of America. Since then the Fourth of July has had several peculiar recognitions. The two men most distinguished in the framing and support of the Declaration were Thomas Jefferson and John Adams—the one having penned it, and the other sustained it the most forcibly in debate—the only two of the fifty-five who signed it that were elected Presidents of the United States. Precisely fifty years after they put their hands to the paper, it pleased Almighty God to take both from this stage of action. This was indeed an extraordinary and remarkable event in our history. Another president, five years after, was called from this stage of existence on the same day and month of the year; and now on this last Fourth of July just passed, when we have a gigantic rebellion, at the bottom of which is an effort to overthrow the principle that all men are created equal, we have the surrender of a most powerful position and army on that very day. . . . Gentlemen, this is a glorious theme, and the occasion for a speech, but I am not prepared to make one worthy of the occasion. I would like to speak in terms of praise due to the many brave officers and soldiers who have fought in the cause of the Union and liberties of their country from the beginning of the war.

(NH IX, 20–21)

December 8, 1863
During the Civil War, President Lincoln advocated a policy of increased immigration as a way to replace the thousands serving in the military.

The condition of the several organized Territories is generally satisfactory although Indian disturbances in New Mexico have not been entirely suppressed. The mineral resources of Colorado, Nevada, Idaho, New Mexico, and Arizona are proving far richer than has been heretofore understood. I lay before you a communication on this subject from the governor of New Mexico. I again subject to your consideration the expediency of establishing a system for the encouragement of immigration. Although this source of national wealth and strength is again flowing with greater freedom than for several years before the insurrection occurred, there is still a great deficiency of laborers in every field of industry, especially in agriculture, and in our mines, as well of iron and coal as of the precious metals. While the demand for labor is thus increased here, tens of thousands of persons, destitute of remunerative occupation, are thronging our foreign consulates, and offering to emigrate to the United States if essential, but very cheap, assistance can be afforded them. It is easy to see that, under the sharp discipline of civil war, the nation is beginning a new life. This noble effort demands the aid, and ought to receive the attention and support of the government.

(NH IX, 230–31)

December 8, 1863
Government policy toward Native Americans on the American frontier, from the annual message to Congress.

The measures provided at your last session for the removal of certain Indian tribes have been carried into effect. Sundry treaties have been negotiated, which will, in due time, be submitted for the constitutional action of the Senate. They contain stipulations for extinguishing the possessory rights of the Indians to large and valuable tracts of land. It is hoped that the effect of these treaties will result in the establishment of permanent friendly relations with such of these tribes as have been brought into frequent and bloody collision with our outlying settlements and emigrants. Sound policy, and our imperative duty to these wards of the government, demand our anxious and constant attention to their material wellbeing, to their progress in the arts of civilization, and, above all, to that moral training which, under the blessing of Divine Providence, will confer upon them the elevated and sanctifying influences, the hopes and consolations, of the Christian faith.

(NH IX, 243)

April 18, 1864
From a speech in Baltimore, Maryland.

The world has never had a good definition of the word liberty, and the American people, just now, are much in want of one. We all declare for liberty; but in using the same word we do not all mean the same thing. With some the word liberty may mean for each man to do as he pleases with himself, and the product of his labor; while with others the same word may mean for some men to do as they please with other men, and the product of other men's labor. Here are two, not only different, but incompatible things, called by the same name, liberty. And it follows that each of the things is, by the respective parties, called by the two different and incompatible names—liberty and tyranny.

(NH X, 77)

Legislator and Congressman

Though he was defeated in his first attempt at elected office, Lincoln went on to a highly successful political career. He served four terms in the Illinois legislature, where he became the floor leader, and in 1846 was elected as the Whig candidate for Congress. Disillusioned by his inability to secure a prominent position in President Zachary Taylor's administration, Lincoln dropped out of politics in 1849 and returned to his law practice. When Stephen A. Douglas succeeded in having the Missouri Compromise repealed in 1852, Lincoln returned to politics with a renewed sense of mission.

March 9, 1832
From an address to the people of Sangamon County, during Lincoln's bid to become an Illinois assemblyman.

That the poorest and most thinly populated countries would be greatly benefited by the opening of good roads, and in the clearing of navigable streams within their limit, is what no person will deny. Yet it is folly to undertake works of this or any other kind without first knowing that we are able to finish them, as half-finished work generally proves to be labor lost.

(NH I, 1)

March 9, 1832
From an address to the people of Sangamon County.

Every man is said to have his peculiar ambition. Whether it be true or not, I can say, for one, that I have no other so great as that of being truly esteemed of my fellow-men, by rendering myself worthy of their esteem. How far I shall succeed in gratifying this ambition, is yet to be developed. I am young, and unknown to many of you. I was born and have ever remained in the most humble walks of life. I have no wealthy or popular relations or friends to recommend me. My case is thrown exclusively upon the independent voters of the country, and if elected they will have conferred a favor upon me, for which I shall be unremitting in my labors to compensate. But if the good people in their wisdom shall see fit to keep me in the background, I have been too familiar with disappointments to be very much chagrined.

(CW I, 8–9)

February 14, 1843
After serving for four terms in the Illinois legislature, Lincoln began lobbying for the Whig nomination for Congress.

Now if you should hear any one say that Lincoln don't want to go to Congress, I wish you as a personal friend of mine, would tell him you have reason to believe he is mistaken. The truth is, I would like to go very much. Still, circumstances may happen which may prevent my being a candidate.

If there are any who be my friends in such an enterprise, what I now want is that they shall not throw me away just yet.

(CW I, 307)

March 26, 1843
Lincoln was one of two contenders for the Whig nomination, but was not selected.

It would astonish, if not amuse, the older citizens to learn that I (a stranger, friendless, uneducated, penniless boy, working on a flatboat at ten dollars per month) have been put down here as the candidate of pride, wealth, and aristocratic family distinction. Yet so, chiefly, it was. There was, too, the strangest combination of church influence against me. . . . My wife has some relations in the Presbyterian churches, and some with the Episcopal churches; and therefore, wherever it would tell, I was set down as either the one or the other, while it was everywhere contended that no Christian ought to go for me, because I belonged to no church, was suspected of being a deist, and had talked about fighting a duel.

(NH I, 262–63)

January 8, 1848
Letter to William Herndon, shortly after making a political
speech.

As to speech-making, by way of getting the hang of the House I made a little speech two or three days ago on a post-office question of no general interest. I find speaking here and elsewhere about the same thing. I was about as badly scared, and no worse, as I am when I speak in court.

(NH I, 325)

June 5, 1850
Letter to the editors of the Illinois Journal, *after Lincoln had left*
politics to devote time to his law practice.

An article in the Tazewell Mirror in which my name is prominently used, makes me fear that my position, with reference to the next Congressional election in this district, is misunderstood, and that such misunderstanding may work injury to the cause of our friends. I therefore take occasion to say that I neither seek, expect, or desire a nomination for a seat in the next Congress; that I prefer my name should not be brought forward in that connection; and that I would now peremptorily forbid the use of it, could I feel entirely at liberty to do so. I will add, that in my opinion, the Whigs of the district have several other men, any one of whom they can elect, and that too quite as easily as they could elect me.

(CW II, 79)

November 10, 1854
After being elected to the Illinois legislature on November 7,
Lincoln declined his seat and began gathering support for a U.S.
Senate bid.

You used to express a good deal of partiality for me; and if you are
still so, now is the time. Some friends here are really for me, for
the U.S. Senate; and I should be very grateful if you could make a
mark for me among your members. Please write me at all events,
giving me the names, post offices, and political position of members around you.

(CW II, 286)

February 9, 1855
The Illinois legislature defeats Lincoln's bid for the U.S. Senate,
despite getting the largest number of votes.

The agony is over at last; and the result you doubtless know. . . . I
regret my defeat moderately, but I am not nervous about it.

(CW II, 305–06)

February 21, 1855
On February 8, Lincoln was defeated by Lyman Trumbull in a
bid to become a U.S. Senator.

The election is over, the session is ended, and I am not Senator. I
have to content myself with the honor of having been the first
choice of a large majority of the fifty-one members who finally
made the election.

(CW II, 306)

December 1856
Lincoln was disillusioned when he lost the Senate election to
Trumbull.

With me, the race of ambition has been a failure—a flat failure;
with him it has been one of splendid success. His name fills the

nation; and is not unknown, even, in foreign lands. I affect no contempt for the high eminence he has reached. So reached, that the oppressed of my species, might have shared with me in the elevation, I would rather stand on that eminence, than wear the richest crown that ever pressed a monarch's brow.

(CW II, 383)

July 10, 1858
Lincoln often used self-deprecating humor to political advantage, as he did when he countered Stephen Douglas's claim that Lincoln was stirring up sectional controversy with his "House Divided" speech.

Gentlemen, reading from speeches is a very tedious business, particularly for an old man who has to put on spectacles, and more so if the man be so tall that he has to bend over to the light. . . . I am not a master of language; I have not a fine education; I am not capable of entering into a disquisition upon dialectics, as I believe you call it; but I do not believe the language I employed bears any such construction as Judge Douglas puts upon it.

(NH III, 32)

July 17, 1858
During a speech in Springfield.

Nobody has ever expected me to be president. In my poor, lean, lank face nobody has ever seen that any cabbages were sprouting out. . . . I am, in a certain sense, made the standard-bearer in behalf of the Republicans. I was made so merely because there had to be someone so placed, I being in no wise preferable to any other one of the twenty-five, perhaps a hundred, we have in the Republican ranks.

(NH III, 158)

July 29, 1858
In a subsequent bid to become a U.S. Senator, Lincoln challenged Stephen A. Douglas, his Democratic rival and a staunch defender

of the Kansas-Nebraska Act, to a series of seven debates. Held in seven cities throughout Illinois, the published Lincoln-Douglas debates propelled Lincoln into national prominence.

I agree to an arrangement for us to speak at the seven places you have named, and at your own times, provided you name the times at once, so that I, as well as you, can have to myself the time not covered by the arrangements. As to the other details, I wish perfect reciprocity, and no more. I wish as much time as you, and that conclusions shall alternate.

(NH III, 195–96)

August 14, 1858
As the date of their first debate approached, Stephen A. Douglas made a public comment that he could best Lincoln in a fight, no matter of what sort. Lincoln replied in a typically humorous fashion.

I am informed that my distinguished friend yesterday became a little excited, nervous perhaps, and he said something about fighting, as though referring to a pugilistic encounter between him and myself. . . . I am informed, further, that somebody in his audience, rather more excited, or nervous, than himself, took off his coat, and offered to take the job off Judge Douglas' hands. . . . Well, I merely desire to say that I shall fight neither Judge Douglas nor his second. I shall not do this for two reasons, which I will now explain. In the first place, a fight would prove nothing which is in issue in this contest. It might establish that Judge Douglas is a more muscular man than myself, or it might demonstrate that I am a more muscular man than Judge Douglas. But this question is not referred to in the Cincinnati platform, nor in either of the Springfield platforms. Neither result would prove him right or me wrong. And so of the gentleman who volunteered to do his fighting for him. If my fighting Judge Douglas would not prove anything, it would certainly prove nothing for me to fight his bottle-holder. My second reason for not having a personal encounter with the Judge is that I don't believe he wants it himself. He and I are about the best friends in the world, and when we get together he would no more think of fighting me than of fighting his wife.

(CW II, 541–42)

August 22, 1858
From a letter written shortly after the first Lincoln-Douglas debate.

Douglas and I, for the first time this canvass, crossed swords here yesterday; the fire flew some, and I am glad to know I am yet alive. There was a vast concourse of people—more than could get near enough to hear.

(CW III, 37)

September 15, 1858
Lincoln's reply to Stephen Douglas's assertion that Lincoln had been "laid up seven days" after their second debate.

Judge Douglas, when he made that statement, must have been crazy, and wholly out of his sober senses, or else he would have known that, when he got me down here, that promise—that windy promise—of his powers to annihilate me wouldn't amount to anything. Now, how little do I look like being carried away trembling? . . . Did the judge talk of trotting me down to Egypt to scare me to death? Why, I know this people better than he does. I was raised just a little east of here. I am a part of this people. But the judge was raised further north, and perhaps he has some horrid idea of what this people might be induced to do.

(NH IV, 68–69)

October 13, 1858
A comment made during the sixth debate with Stephen Douglas.

He asks me, or he asks the audience, if I wish to push this matter to the point of personal difficulty. I tell him, no. He did not make a mistake, in one of his early speeches, when he called me an "amiable" man, though perhaps he did when he called me an "intelligent" man. It really hurts me very much to suppose that I have wronged anybody on earth. I again tell him, no! I very much prefer, when this canvass shall be over, however it may result, that we at least part without any bitter recollections of personal difficulties.

(NH IV, 327)

October 20, 1858
Lincoln was concerned that a scheme to bring illegal voters into Illinois might cause him to lose his bid for the Senate.

I have now a high degree of confidence that we shall succeed, if we are not overrun with fraudulent votes to a greater extent than usual. On alighting from the cars and walking three squares at Naples on Monday, I met about fifteen Celtic gentlemen, with black carpet-sacks in their hands.

I learned that they had crossed over from the railroad in Brown County, but where they were going no one could tell. They dropped in about the doggeries, and were still hanging about when I left. At Brown County yesterday I was told that about four hundred of the same sort were to be brought into Schuyler, before the election, to work on some new railroad; but on reaching here I find [John C.] Bagby thinks that is not so. What I most dread is that they will introduce into the doubtful districts numbers of men who are legal voters in all respects except residence and who will swear to residence and thus put it beyond our power to exclude them. They can and I fear will swear falsely on that point, because they know it is next to impossible to convict them of perjury upon it.

(CW III, 329–30)

October 30, 1858
Part of a speech in Springfield, Illinois, during Lincoln's failed run for the Senate.

I have meant to assail the motives of no party, or individual; and if I have, in any instance (of which I am not conscious) departed from my purpose, I regret it.

I have said that in some respects the contest has been painful to me. Myself, and those with whom I act have been constantly accused of a purpose to destroy the Union; and bespattered with every imaginable odious epithet; and some who were friends, as it were but yesterday have made themselves most active in this. I have cultivated patience, and made no attempt at a retort.

(CW III, 334)

November 19, 1858
From a letter written after Lincoln lost the Senate election to Stephen A. Douglas.

I am glad I made the late race. It gave me a hearing on the great and durable question of the age, which I could have had in no other way; and though I now sink out of view, and shall be forgotten, I believe I have made some marks which will tell for the cause of civil liberty long after I am gone.

(CW III, 339)

November 19, 1858
Despite losing the election, Lincoln was determined to keep fighting.

Well, the election is over; and, in the main point, we are beaten. Still, my view is that the fight must go on. Let no one falter. The question is not half settled. New splits and divisions will soon be upon our adversaries; and we shall have fun again.

(CW III, 340)

March 26, 1859
To the publisher of the Lincoln-Douglas debates.

Judge Douglas would have the right to correct typographical errors in his, if he desired; but I think the necessity, in his case, would be less than in mine; because he had two hired reporters traveling with him, and probably revised their manuscripts before they went to press; while I had no reporter of my own, but depended on a very excellent one sent by the Press & Tribune; but who never waited to show me his notes or manuscripts; so that the first I saw of my speeches, after delivering them, was in the Press & Tribune precisely as they now stand.

(CW III, 373)

September 16, 1859
From a speech in Columbus, Ohio, where Stephen Douglas had spoken earlier.

I feel that it will be well for you, as for me, that you should not raise your expectations to that standard to which you would have been justified in raising them had one of these distinguished men appeared before you. You would perhaps be only preparing a disappointment for yourselves, and, as a consequence of your disappointment, mortification to me. I hope, therefore, that you will commence with very moderate expectations; and perhaps, if you will give me your attention, I shall be able to interest you to a moderate degree.

(NH V, 140–41)

September 17, 1859
From a speech in Cincinnati, Ohio.

This is the first time in my life that I have appeared before an audience in so great a city as this. I therefore—though I am no longer a young man—make this appearance under some degree of embarrassment. But I have found that when one is embarrassed, usually the shortest way to get through with it is to quit talking or thinking about it, and go at something else.

(NH V, 190)

December 14, 1859
To a Republican official, regarding Lincoln's work for the party.

As to that matter about the Committee, in relation to appointing delegates by general convention, or by districts, I shall attend to it as well as I know how, which, G_d knows, will not be very well.

(CW III, 509)

December 20, 1859
An account of Lincoln's political career, supplied for biographical literature.

I went the campaign, was elected, ran for the legislature the same year (1832), and was beaten—the only time I ever have been beaten by the people. The next and three succeeding biennial elections I was elected to the legislature. I was not a candidate afterward. During this legislative period I had studied law, and removed to Springfield to practice it. In 1846 I was once elected to the Lower House of Congress. Was not a candidate for reelection. From 1848 to 1854, both inclusive, practiced law more assiduously than ever before. Always a Whig in politics; and generally on the Whig electoral tickets, making active canvasses. I was losing interest in politics when the repeal of the Missouri Compromise aroused me again. What I have done since then is pretty well known.

(NH V, 288)

President

The Lincoln–Douglas debates propelled Lincoln onto the national stage. Shortly after the debates were published, he received the Republican nomination for president. Lincoln became the sixteenth president after one of the most contentious and bitterly fought elections in American history. The Civil War began just one month after he took office. Lincoln was widely reviled in the South, and in the North; the perception that he was not prosecuting the war successfully almost derailed his chance at a second term. Five days after General Lee surrendered at Appomattox, Virginia, and only one month into his second term, Lincoln was assassinated by John Wilkes Booth.

July 25, 1858
From a eulogy for President Zachary Taylor.

The presidency, even to the most experienced politicians, is no bed of roses; and Gen. Taylor like others, found thorns within it. No human being can fill that station and escape censure.

(CW II, 89)

April 16, 1859
From a letter to a newspaper editor who wanted to publish Lincoln's name as a presidential candidate, not long after Lincoln lost his bid for the Senate.

As for the other matter you kindly mention, I must in candor say I do not think myself fit for the presidency. I certainly am flattered and gratified that some partial friends think of me in that connection; but I really think it best for our cause that no concerted effort, such as you suggest, should be made.

(NH V, 127–28)

September 6, 1859
Letter to Samuel Galloway.

I must say I do not think myself fit for the presidency.

(NH V, 138)

December 14, 1859
Lincoln's name was first suggested for the presidency in November 1858, after losing his bid for the Senate to Stephen A. Douglas.

You know I am pledged to not enter a struggle with him for the seat in the Senate now occupied by him; and yet I would rather have a full term in the Senate than in the presidency.

(NH V, 282)

February 27, 1860
Comment directed at Southern secessionists during an address at the Cooper Institute, New York.

You will not abide the election of a Republican president! In that supposed event, you say, you will destroy the Union; and then, you say, the great crime of having destroyed it will be upon us! That is cool. A highwayman holds a pistol to my ear, and mutters through his teeth, "Stand and deliver, or I shall kill you, and then you will be a murderer!"

(NH V, 323)

March 6, 1860
Before he won the Republican nomination, Lincoln used his humble origins to win supporters in Hartford, Connecticut. He was advertised as "the rail splitter" candidate in the presidential election.

I am not ashamed to confess that twenty-five years ago I was a hired laborer, mauling rails, at work on a flatboat—just what might happen to any poor man's son.

(NH V, 361)

March 17, 1860
Note regarding Lincoln's chances of getting the Republican nomination for president.

I could not raise ten thousand dollars if it would save me from the fate of John Brown. Nor have my friends, so far as I know, yet reached the point of staking any money on my chances of success.

(NH VI, 7)

March 24, 1860
Lincoln on his strategy for securing the nomination.

If I have any chance, it consists mainly in the fact that the whole opposition would vote for me if nominated. (I don't mean to include the pro-slavery opposition of the South, of course.) My name is new in the field; and I suppose I am not the first choice of a very great many. Our policy, then, is to give no offense to others—leave them in a mood to come to us, if they shall be compelled to give up their first love. This, too, is dealing justly with all, and leaving us in a mood to support heartily whoever shall be nominated.

(CW IV, 34)

April 29, 1860
To Lyman Trumbull, who asked Lincoln whether he had the desire to be president.

The taste is in my mouth a little; and this, no doubt, disqualifies me, to some extent, to form correct opinions.

(CW IV, 45)

May 2, 1860
As the nomination progressed, Lincoln became increasingly opti-
mistic that he would be selected.

First, then, I think the Illinois delegation will be unanimous for
me at the start; and no other delegation will. A few individuals in
other delegations would like to go for me at the start, but may be
restrained by their colleagues. It is represented to me, by men who
ought to know, that the whole of Indiana might not be difficult to
get. You know how it is in Ohio. I am certainly not the first choice
there; and yet I have not heard that anyone makes any positive objection to me. It is just so everywhere so far as I can perceive.

(CW IV, 47)

May 21, 1860
On May 6, 1860, Lincoln received his party's nomination.

Deeply and even painfully sensible of the great responsibility
which is inseparable from this high honor—a responsibility which
I could almost wish had fallen upon some one of the far more eminent men and experienced statesmen whose distinguished names
were before the convention—I shall, by your leave, consider more
fully the resolutions of the convention, denominated the platform,
and without any unnecessary or unreasonable delay respond to
you, Mr. Chairman, in writing, not doubting that the platform
will be found satisfactory, and the nomination gratefully accepted.

(NH VI, 13)

May 21, 1860
From a letter to a supporter.

I am not wanting in the purpose, though I may fail in the
strength, to maintain my freedom from bad influences. . . . May
the Almighty grant that the cause of truth, justice, and humanity
shall in no wise suffer at my hands.

(NH VI, 14)

May 23, 1860
An extract from Lincoln's acceptance letter to George Ashmun,
president of the Republican convention.

Imploring the assistance of Divine Providence, and with due regard to the views and feelings of all who were represented in the convention; to the rights of all the states, and territories, and people of the nation; to the inviolability of the Constitution, and the perpetual union, harmony, and prosperity of all, I am most happy to cooperate for the practical success of the principles declared by the convention.

(CW IV, 52)

July 18, 1860
Note to Lincoln's eventual vice president, Hannibal Hamlin.

It appears to me that you and I ought to be acquainted, and accordingly I write this as a sort of introduction of myself to you. You first entered the Senate during the single term I was a member of the House of Representatives, but I have no recollection that we were introduced. I shall be pleased to receive a line from you.

(CW IV, 84)

August 4, 1860
During the presidential race, Southern votes were split between
three Democratic contenders, thus ensuring Lincoln's election.

I hesitate to say it, but it really appears now, as if the success of the Republican ticket is inevitable. We have no reason to doubt any of the states which voted for Fremont. Add to these, Minnesota, Pennsylvania, and New Jersey, and the thing is done. Minnesota is as sure as such a thing can be; while the democracy are so divided between Douglas and Breckenridge in Pennsylvania and New Jersey that they are scarcely less sure. Our friends are also confident in Indiana and Illinois. I should expect the same division would give us a fair chance in Oregon.

(CW IV, 90)

August 8, 1860
In Springfield, Illinois, Lincoln acknowledged a group of well-
wishers at a large Republican rally.

I am profoundly gratified for this manifestation of your feelings. I
am gratified, because it is a tribute such as can be paid to no man
as a man. It is the evidence that four years from this time you will
give a like manifestation to the next man who is the representative
of the truth on the questions that now agitate the public. And it is
because you will then fight for this cause as you do now, or with
even greater ardor than now, though I be dead and gone.

(CW IV, 91)

September 1, 1860
To Senator Henry Wilson from Massachusetts.

The point you press—the importance of thorough organization—
is felt, and appreciated by our friends everywhere. And yet it in-
volves so much more of dry, and irksome labor, that most of them
shrink from it—preferring parades, and shows, and monster meet-
ings. I know not how this can be helped. I do what I can in my position, for organization; but it does not amount to so much as it
should.

(CW IV, 109)

October 19, 1860
During the presidential election, a young girl wrote to ask
Lincoln about his family, and to say that growing a beard "would
look a great deal better for your face is so thin. All the ladies like
whiskers and they tease their husbands to vote for you and then
you would be president."

I regret the necessity of saying I have no daughters. I have three
sons—one seventeen, one nine, and one seven years of age. They,
with their mother, constitute my whole family.

As to the whiskers, having never worn any, do you not think

people would call it a piece of silly affectation if I were to begin now?

(CW IV, 129–30)

October 29, 1860
Many citizens wrote to ask Lincoln for a clarification of his policies.

I have bad men to deal with, both North and South; men who are eager for something new upon which to base new misrepresentations; men who would like to frighten me, or at least to fix upon me the character of timidity and cowardice. . . . I intend keeping my eye upon these gentlemen, and to not unnecessarily put any weapons in their hands.

(NH VI, 67)

November 6, 1860
A note to Vice President Hannibal Hamlin, the day after Lincoln was elected president.

I am anxious for a personal interview with you at as early a day as possible. Can you, without much inconvenience, meet me at Chicago?

(CW IV, 136)

November 20, 1860
From a speech shortly after Lincoln was elected president.

I thank you in common with all those who have thought fit by their votes to indorse the Republican cause. I rejoice with you in the success which has thus far attended that cause. Yet in all our rejoicings, let us neither express nor cherish any hard feelings toward any citizen who by his vote has differed with us. Let us at all times remember that all American citizens dwell together in the bonds of fraternal feeling.

(NH VI, 72)

December 15, 1860
President Lincoln refused to change his policies.

Is it desired that I shall shift the ground upon which I have been elected? I cannot do it.

(NH VI, 79)

January 3, 1861
William Seward wrote to warn Lincoln of a possible Confederate attack on Washington.

It seems to me the inauguration is not the most dangerous point for us. Our adversaries have us more clearly at disadvantage, on the second Wednesday of February, when the votes should be officially counted. If the two Houses refuse to meet at all, or meet without a quorum of each, where shall we be? I do not think this counting is constitutionally essential to the election; but how are we to proceed in absence of it?

(CW IV, 170)

February 11, 1861
Shortly before leaving for his inauguration, Lincoln delivered a farewell speech to the citizens of Springfield, Illinois.

My friends: no one, not in my situation, can appreciate my feeling of sadness at this parting. To this place, and the kindness of these people, I owe everything. Here I have lived a quarter of a century, and have passed from a young to an old man. Here my children have been born, and one is buried. I now leave, not knowing when or whether ever I may return, with a task before me greater than that which rested upon Washington. Without the assistance of that Divine Being who ever attended him, I cannot succeed. With that assistance, I cannot fail.

(NH VI, 110)

February 11, 1861
Remarks delivered as Lincoln was traveling to his inauguration.

I am leaving you on an errand of national importance, attended, as you are aware, with considerable difficulties. Let us believe, as some poet expressed it: Behind the cloud the sun is still shining.

(CW IV, 191)

February 11, 1861
President-elect Lincoln addressed the concerns of citizens as he traveled to Washington.

In all the trying positions in which I shall be placed, and doubtless I shall be placed in many trying ones, my reliance will be upon you and the people of the United States—and I wish you to remember now and forever, that it is your business, and not mine; that if the union of these states and liberties of this people shall be lost, it is but little to any one man of fifty-two years of age, but a great deal to the thirty millions of people who inhabit these United States, and to their posterity in all coming time. It is your business to rise up and preserve the Union and liberty, for yourselves, and not for me. I desire they shall be constitutionally preserved.

I, as already intimated, am but an accidental instrument, temporary, and to serve but for a limited time, but I appeal to you again to constantly bear in mind that with you, and not with politicians, not with presidents, not with office-seekers, but with you, is the question: "Shall the Union and shall the liberties of this country be preserved to the latest generations?"

(CW IV, 194)

February 14, 1861
Remarks from an impromptu speech as Lincoln was traveling to his inauguration.

Though the majority may be wrong, and I will not undertake to say that they were not wrong in electing me, yet we must adhere to the principle that the majority shall rule. By your Constitution you have another chance in four years. No great harm can be done by us in that time—in that time there can be nobody hurt. If anything goes wrong, however, and you find you have made a mistake, elect a better man next time. There are plenty of them.

(CW IV, 207)

February 18, 1861
In front of the New York legislature, President-elect Lincoln spoke of the difficult job ahead.

It is true that, while I hold myself, without mock modesty, the humblest of all individuals that have ever been elevated to the presidency, I have a more difficult task to perform than any one of them.

(NH VI, 140)

February 19, 1861
Comment made on the road to Lincoln's inauguration.

I do not say that in the recent election the people did the wisest thing that could have been done; indeed, I do not think that they did; but do say that in accepting the great trust committed to me, which I do with a determination to endeavor to prove worthy of it, I must rely upon you, upon the people of the whole country, for support; and with their sustaining aid, even I, humble as I am, cannot fail to carry the ship of state safely through the storm.

(NH VI, 143–44)

February 19, 1861
From the address to the New York legislature.

I have been occupying a position, since the presidential election, of silence—of avoiding public speaking, of avoiding public writing. I have been doing so because I thought, upon full consideration, that was the proper course for me to take. . . . I have not kept silence since the presidential election from any party wantonness, or from any indifference to the anxiety that pervades the minds of men about the aspect of the political affairs of this country. I have kept silence for the reason that I supposed it was peculiarly proper that I should do so until the time came when, according to the custom of the country, I could speak officially.

(NH VI, 146–47)

February 20, 1861
Reply to the mayor of New York City.

In my devotion to the Union, I hope I am behind no man in the nation. As to my wisdom in conducting affairs so as to tend to the preservation of the Union, I fear too great confidence may have been placed in me. I am sure I bring a heart devoted to the work.

(NH VI, 149)

February 21, 1861
From an address to the New Jersey Assembly.

I appropriate to myself very little of the demonstrations of respect with which I have been greeted. I think little should be given to any man, but that it should be a manifestation of adherence to the Union and the Constitution. I understand myself to be received here by the representatives of the people of New Jersey, a majority of whom differ in opinion from those with whom I have acted. This manifestation is therefore to be regarded by me as expressing their devotion to the Union, the Constitution, and the liberties of the people.

(NH VI, 152–53)

February 21, 1861
From a reply to the mayor of Philadelphia.

The hope that has been expressed by your mayor, that I may be able to restore peace, harmony, and prosperity to the country, is most worthy of him; and most happy, indeed, will I be if I shall be able to verify and fulfill that hope. I promise you that I bring to the work a sincere heart. Whether I will bring a head equal to that heart will be for future times to determine.

(NH VI, 155)

March 4, 1861
On the day of his inauguration, Lincoln asked Republican Senator William Seward, a powerful political rival from New York, to head the Department of State. When Seward declined, Lincoln begged him to reconsider, and Seward finally relented.

Your note . . . asking to withdraw your acceptance of my invitation . . . was duly received. It is the subject of the most painful solicitude with me, and I feel constrained to beg that you will countermand the withdrawal. The public interest, I think, demands that you should; and my personal feelings are deeply enlisted in the same direction. Please consider and answer by 9 A.M. tomorrow.

(NH VI, 185)

March 4, 1861
A passage from Lincoln's first inaugural address, in which he attempted to placate his Southern constituents. (See Appendix C for complete text.)

Apprehension seems to exist among the people of the Southern states that by the accession of a Republican administration their property and their peace and personal security are to be endangered. There has never been any reasonable cause for such apprehension. Indeed, the most ample evidence to the contrary has all the while existed and been open to their inspection. It is found in nearly all the published speeches of him who now addresses you. I do but quote from one of those speeches when I declare that "I have no purpose, directly or indirectly, to interfere with the institution of slavery in the states where it exists. I believe I have no lawful right to do so, and I have no inclination to do so." Those who nominated and elected me did so with full knowledge that I had made this and many similar declarations, and had never recanted them.

(NH VI, 169–70)

March 4, 1861
From Lincoln's first inaugural address.

I therefore consider that, in view of the Constitution and the laws, the Union is unbroken; and to the extent of my ability I shall take care, as the Constitution itself expressly enjoins upon me, that the laws of the Union be faithfully executed in all the states. Doing this I deem to be only a simple duty on my part; and I shall perform it so far as practicable, unless my rightful masters, the American people, shall withhold the requisite means, or in some authoritative manner direct the contrary. I trust this will not be regarded as a menace, but only as the declared purpose of the Union that it will constitutionally defend and maintain itself.

(NH VI, 175)

March 4, 1861
From Lincoln's first inaugural address.

The chief magistrate derives all his authority from the people, and they have conferred none upon him to fix terms for the separation of the states. The people themselves can do this also if they choose; but the executive, as such, has nothing to do with it. His duty is to administer the present government, as it came to his hands, and to transmit it, unimpaired by him, to his successor.

(NH VI, 183)

March 4, 1861
From Lincoln's first inaugural address.

By the frame of the government under which we live, this same people have wisely given their public servants but little power for mischief; and have, with equal wisdom provided for the return of that little to their own hands at very short intervals. While the people retain their virtue and vigilance, no administration, by any extreme of wickedness or folly, can very seriously injure the government in the short space of four years.

(NH VI, 183–84)

July 4, 1861
Shortly after the onset of the Civil War, President Lincoln de-scribed the state of foreign relations to a special session of Congress.

The forbearance of this government has been so extraordinary and so long continued as to lead some foreign nations to shape their action as if they supposed the early destruction of our national union was probable. While this, on discovery, gave the executive some concern, he is now happy to say that the sovereignty and rights of the United States are now everywhere practically respected by foreign powers; and a general sympathy with the country is manifested throughout the world.

(NH VI, 311)

August 1, 1861
President Lincoln wrote to the tycoon of Japan requesting that ports be opened to American trade.

I have received the letter which you have addressed to me on the subject of a desired extension of the time stipulated by treaty for the opening of certain ports and cities in Japan. The question is surrounded with many difficulties. While it is my earnest desire to consult the convenience of your Majesty, and to accede, so far as I can, to your reasonable wishes, so kindly expressed, the interests of the United States must, nevertheless, have due consideration.

(NH VI, 336)

October 11, 1861
Letter to the viceroy of Egypt, concerning a case involving an American missionary.

I have received from Mr. Thayer, consul-general of the United States at Alexandria, a full account of the liberal, enlightened, and energetic proceedings which, on his complaint, you have adopted in bringing to speedy and condign punishment the parties, subjects of your highness in Upper Egypt, who were concerned in an act of criminal persecution against Faris, an agent of certain Christian missionaries in Upper Egypt.

(NH VII, 7)

October 17, 1861
Many citizens applied directly to President Lincoln for work.

The lady bearer of this says she has two sons who want to work. Set them at it if possible. Wanting to work is so rare a want that it should be encouraged.

(NH XI, 120)

November 21, 1861
Lincoln admired Horace Greeley, an antislavery spokesman who wrote for the New York Tribune.

I need not tell you that I have the highest confidence in Mr. Greeley. He is a great power. Having him firmly behind me will be as helpful as an army of one hundred thousand men.

(NH XI, 121)

January 22, 1862
President Lincoln received many death threats, but resisted Secretary Stanton's wish to have him protected by a bodyguard.

On reflection I think it will not do, as a rule, for the adjutant-general to attend me wherever I go: not that I have any objection to his presence, but that it would be an uncompensating encumbrance both to him and me. When it shall occur to me to go anywhere, I wish to be free to go at once, and not to have to notify the adjutant-general and wait till he can get ready.

(NH VII, 87)

September 13, 1862
Lincoln received unsolicited advice from many quarters, including religious groups.

I am approached with the most opposite opinions and advice, and that by religious men who are equally certain that they represent the divine will. I am sure that either the one or the other class is mistaken in that belief, and perhaps in some respects both. I hope it will not be irreverent for me to say that if it is probable that God would reveal his will to others on a point so connected with duty, it might be supposed he would reveal it directly to me; for, unless I am more deceived in myself than I often am, it is my earnest desire to know the will of Providence in this matter. And if I can learn what it is, I will do it.

(NH VIII, 28–29)

September 28, 1862
Though public response to the Emancipation Proclamation was generally favorable, Lincoln was dissatisfied with the state of the economy and the dropping rate of enlistments.

It is six days old, and while commendation in newspapers and by distinguished individuals is all that a vain man could wish, the stocks have declined, and troops come forward more slowly than ever. This, looked soberly in the face, is not very satisfactory. We have fewer troops in the field at the end of six days than we had at the beginning—the attrition among the old outnumbering the addition by the new. The North responds to the proclamation sufficiently in breath; but breath alone kills no rebels.

(NH VIII, 50)

December 1, 1862
A report of improvements in communication infrastructure, from the annual message to Congress.

I have favored the project for connecting the United States with Europe by an Atlantic telegraph, and a similar project to extend

the telegraph from San Francisco, to connect by a Pacific telegraph with the line which is being extended across the Russian
empire.

(NH VIII, 99)

December 1, 1862
President Lincoln's report on transportation improvements, from
the annual message to Congress.

I submit a statement of the proceedings of commissioners, which
shows the progress that has been made in the enterprise of con-
structing the Pacific Railroad. And this suggests the earliest completion of this road, and also the favorable action of Congress
upon the projects now pending before them for enlarging the ca-
pacities of the great canals in New York and Illinois, as being of
vital and rapidly increasing importance to the whole nation, and
especially to the vast interior region hereinafter to be noticed at
some greater length.

(NH VIII, 108–09)

December 1, 1862
In 1862, the Department of Agriculture was created, but without
cabinet status.

I have caused the Department of Agriculture of the United States
to be organized. The commissioner informs me that within the
period of a few months this department has established an extensive system of correspondence and exchanges, both at home and
abroad, which promises to effect highly beneficial results in the
development of a correct knowledge of recent improvements in
agriculture, the introduction of new products, and in the collection of the agricultural statistics of the different states.

(NH VIII, 109)

June 29, 1863
President Lincoln responded to a group who challenged the legal-
ity of his decision to suspend the writ of habeas corpus at several
points during the Civil War.

You ask, in substance, whether I really claim that I may override all guaranteed rights of individuals, on the plea of conserving the public safety—when I may choose to say the public safety requires it. This question, divested of the phraseology calculated to represent me as struggling for an arbitrary personal prerogative, is either simply a question who shall decide, or an affirmation that nobody shall decide, what the public safety does require in cases of rebellion or invasion.

The Constitution contemplates the question as likely to occur for decision, but it does not expressly declare who is to decide it. By necessary implication, when rebellion or invasion comes, the decision is to be made from time to time; and I think the man whom, for the time, the people have, under the Constitution, made the commander-in-chief of their army and navy, is the man who holds the power and bears the responsibility of making it. If he uses the power justly, the same people will probably justify him; if he abuses it, he is in their hands to be dealt with by all the modes they have reserved for themselves in the Constitution.

(NH IX, 4)

June 29, 1863
The Democratic Convention in Ohio nominated Clement
Vallandigham, a radical antiwar activist, as their choice for gov-
ernor. Lincoln had him arrested and tried for treason.

When it is known that the whole burden of his speeches has been to stir up men against the prosecution of the war, and that in the midst of resistance to it he has not been known in any instance to counsel against such resistance, it is next to impossible to repel the inference that he has counseled directly in favor of it.

With all this before their eyes, the convention you represent have nominated Mr. Vallandigham for governor of Ohio, and both they and you have declared the purpose to sustain the National Union by all constitutional means. But of course they and you in common reserve to yourselves to decide what are constitutional means; and unlike the Albany meeting, you omit to state or intimate that in your opinion an army is a constitutional means of saving the Union against a rebellion, or even to intimate that you are conscious of an existing rebellion being in progress with the avowed object of destroying that very Union. At the same time your nominee for governor, in whose behalf you appeal, is known to you and to the world to declare against the use of an army to suppress the rebellion. Your own attitude therefore, encourages desertion, resistance to the draft, and the like because it teaches those who incline to desert and to escape the draft to believe it is your purpose to protect them, and to hope that you will become strong enough to do so.

(NH IX, 7–8)

October 5, 1863
Lincoln was forced to contend with conpeting factions in the Republican Party.

The Radicals and the Conservatives each agree with me in some things and disagree in others. I could wish both to agree with me in all things, for then they would agree with each other and would be too strong for any foe from any quarter. They, however, choose to do otherwise; and I do not question their right. I too shall do what seems to be my duty.

(NH IX, 164)

November 2, 1863
From a letter regarding attacks in the press.

My note to you I certainly did not expect to see in print; yet I have not been much shocked by the newspaper comments upon it. Those comments constitute a fair specimen of what has occurred to me through life. I have endured a great deal of ridicule without much malice; and have received a great deal of kindness, not quite free from ridicule. I am used to it.

(NH IX, 199)

April 4, 1864
A comment made at the end of a letter discussing the progress of the war, the emancipation of slaves, and the enlistment of over 100,000 African-Americans into the Union army and navy.

In telling this tale I attempt no compliment to my own sagacity. I claim not to have controlled events, but confess plainly that events have controlled me. Now, at the end of three years' struggle, the nation's condition is not what either party, or any man, devised or expected. God alone can claim it. Whither it is tending seems plain. If God now wills the removal of a great wrong, and wills also that we of the North, as well as you of the South, shall pay fairly for our complicity in that wrong, impartial history will find therein new cause to attest and revere the justice and goodness of God.

(NH X, 68)

May 30, 1864
Appreciation for Republican Congressman Owen Lovejoy, a vocal abolitionist and one of President Lincoln's staunchest supporters.

My personal acquaintance with him just commenced only about ten years ago, since when it has been quite intimate, and every step in it has been one of increasing respect and esteem, ending, with his life, in no less than affection of my part. It can truly be said of him that while he was personally ambitious he bravely endured the obscurity which the unpopularity of his principles imposed, and never accepted official honors until those honors were ready to admit his principles with him. Throughout very heavy and perplexing responsibilities here to the day of his death, it would scarcely wrong any other to say he was my most generous friend.

(NH X, 111)

June 9, 1864
President Lincoln was nominated for a second term at a time when Union victory in the Civil War was still uncertain.

I will neither conceal my gratification nor restrain the expression of my gratitude that the Union people, through their convention, in their continued effort to save and advance the nation, have deemed me not unworthy to remain in my present position.

(NH X, 116–17)

June 9, 1864
On the day after he was nominated for a second term, he made this reply to a delegation from the National Union League.

The part I am entitled to appropriate as a compliment is only that part which I may lay hold of as being the opinion of the convention and of the League, that I am not entirely unworthy to be entrusted with the place which I have occupied for the last three years. But I do not allow myself to suppose that either the convention of the League have concluded to decide that I am either the greatest or best man in America, but rather they have concluded that it is not best to swap horses while crossing the river, and have further concluded that I am not so poor a horse that they might not make a botch of it in trying to swap.

(NH X, 122–23)

July 25, 1864
Letter concerning the upcoming presidential election.

Thus, the presidential contest will almost certainly be no other than a contest between a union and disunion candidate, disunion certainly following the success of the latter. The issue is a mighty one, for all people, and all times; and whoever aids the right will be appreciated and remembered.

(NH X, 171)

August 22, 1864
Address to the 166th Ohio Regiment, which had finished its term of service and was headed home.

I happen, temporarily, to occupy this White House. I am a living witness that any one of your children may look to come here as my father's child has. It is in order that each one of you may have, through this free government which we have enjoyed, an open field and a fair chance for your industry, enterprise, and intelligence; that you may all have equal privileges in the race of life, with all its desirable human aspirations. It is for this the struggle should be maintained, that we may not lose our birthright—not only for one, but for two or three years. The nation is worth fighting for, to secure such an incstimable jewel.

(NH X, 202–03)

August 23, 1864
Based on the mixed successes and failures of his administration during the Civil War, President Lincoln was unsure that he would be elected to a second term.

This morning, as for some days past, it seems exceedingly probable that this administration will not be reelected. Then it will be my duty to so cooperate with the president-elect as to save the Union between the election and the inauguration; as he will have secured his election on such ground that he cannot possibly save it afterward.

(NH X, 203–04)

October 19, 1864
Lincoln's response to a charge that, if he was not reelected, he would attempt to sabotage the government.

I am struggling to maintain the government, not to throw it. I am struggling, especially, to prevent others from overthrowing it. I therefore say that if I shall live I shall remain president until the 4th of next March; and that whoever shall be constitutionally elected therefore, in November, shall be duly installed as president of the 4th of March; and that, in the interval, I shall do my utmost that whoever is to hold the helm for the next voyage shall start with the best possible chance to save the ship.

(NH X, 244)

November 9, 1864
On November 8, 1864, President Lincoln was reelected by an overwhelming majority.

I am thankful to God for this approval of the people; but, while deeply grateful for this mark of their confidence in me, if I know my heart, my gratitude is free from any taint of personal triumph. I do not impugn the motives of anyone opposed to me. It is no pleasure to me to triumph over anyone, but I give thanks to the Almighty for this evidence of the people's resolution to stand by free government and the rights of humanity.

(NH X, 262)

November 10, 1864
Response to a group of well-wishers following Lincoln's reelection.

We cannot have free government without elections; and if the rebellion could force us to forego or postpone a national election, it might fairly claim to have already conquered and ruined us. The strife of the election is but human nature practically applied to the facts of the case. What has occurred in this case must ever recur in similar cases. Human nature will not change. In any future great national trial, compared with the men of this, we shall have as weak and as strong, as silly and as wise, as bad and as good. Let us, therefore, study the incidents of this as philosophy to learn wisdom from, and none of them as wrongs to be revenged. But the election, along with its incidental and undesirable strife, has done good too. It has demonstrated that a people's government can sustain a national election in the midst of a great civil war.

(NH X, 263–64)

March 15, 1865
Lincoln's second inaugural address was short and not well received by the press, but there were some who recognized it as a sublime example of Lincoln's eloquence, including Thurlow Weed. (See Appendix G for complete text.)

Everyone likes a compliment. Thank you for yours on my little notification speech and on the recent inaugural address. I expect the latter to wear as well as—perhaps better than—anything I have produced; but I believe it is not immediately popular. Men are not flattered by being shown that there has been a difference of purpose between the Almighty and them. To deny it, however, in this case, is to deny that there is a God governing the world. It is a truth which I thought needed to be told, and, as whatever humiliation there is in it falls most directly on myself, I thought others might afford for me to tell it.

(NH XI, 54)

April 14, 1865
In Lincoln's last letter, written on the day he was shot, he tried to minimize the threat of assassination. Lincoln died on April 15, 1865.

I intend to adopt the advice of my friends and use due precaution.

(NH XI, 94)

Education

Lincoln grew up with only about one year of formal schooling. He made up for his lack of education by reading voraciously in whatever subjects interested him. As a legislator, Lincoln advocated the expansion of public education, and as president recommended privately that freed slaves be allowed to attend school. Determined that his sons would not suffer the same lack of formal schooling as he always had, he sent both of them to Harvard.

March 9, 1832
In an address to the people of Sangamon County, Lincoln expressed his support for universal education. Lincoln himself had only received about a year of formal schooling.

Upon the subject of education, not presuming to dictate any plan or system respecting it, I can only say that I view it as the most important subject which we as a people can be engaged in. That every man may receive at least a moderate education, and thereby be enabled to read the histories of his own and other countries, by which he may duly appreciate the value of our free institutions, appears to be an object of vital importance, even on this account alone, to say nothing of the advantages and satisfaction to be derived from all being able to read the Scriptures, and other works both of a religious and moral nature, for themselves.

For my part, I desire to see the time when education—and by its means, morality, sobriety, enterprise, and industry—shall become much more general than at present, and should be gratified to have it in my power to contribute something to the advancement of any measure which might have a tendency to accelerate that happy period.

(NH I, 7)

July 16, 1852
An opinion on formal education, from a eulogy for the statesman Henry Clay, whom Lincoln idolized.

Mr. Clay's lack of a more perfect early education, however it may be regretted generally, teaches at least one profitable lesson: it teaches that in this country one can scarcely be so poor but that, if he will, he can acquire sufficient education to get through the world respectably.

(NH II, 160)

February 22, 1859
Lincoln on writing, as told in a speech to the Springfield Library Association.

Writing, the art of communicating thoughts to the mind through the eye, is the great invention of the world. Great is the astonishing range of analysis and combination which necessarily underlies the most crude and general conception of it—great, very great, in enabling us to converse with the dead, the absent, and the unborn, at all distances of time and space; and great, not only in its direct benefits, but greatest help to all other inventions.

(NH V, 107)

February 22, 1859
Lincoln was very interested in the idea of progress.

It is very probable—almost certain—that the great mass of men at that time were utterly unconscious that their condition or their minds were capable of improvement. They not only looked upon the educated few as superior beings, but they supposed themselves to be naturally incapable of rising to equality. To emancipate the mind from this false underestimate of itself is the great task which printing came into the world to perform. It is difficult for us now and here to conceive how strong this slavery of the mind was, and how long it did of necessity take to break its shackles, and to get a habit of freedom of thought established. It is, in this connection, a curious fact that a new country is most favorable—almost necessary—to the emancipation of thought, and the consequent advancement of civilization and the arts.

(NH V, 112)

September 30, 1859
Lincoln on universal education, from a speech to the Wisconsin State Agricultural Society.

As each man has one mouth to be fed, and one pair of hands to furnish food, it was probably intended that that particular pair of hands should feed that particular mouth—that each head is the natural guardian, director, and protector of the hands and mouth inseparably connected with it; and that being so, every head should be cultivated and improved by whatever will add to its capacity for performing its charge. In one word, free labor insists on universal education.

(NH V, 252)

September 30, 1859
Lincoln on reading, from a speech to the Wisconsin State Agricultural Society.

A capacity and taste for reading gives access to whatever has already been discovered by others. It is the key, or one of the keys, to the already solved problems. And not only so: it gives relish and facility for successfully pursuing the unsolved ones.

(NH V, 253)

December 20, 1859
From biographical material supplied for Jesse W. Fell, which was
subsequently printed in various newspapers. (See Appendix B for
complete text.)

My father, at the death of his father, was but six years of age, and he grew up literally without education. . . . There were some schools, so called, but no qualification was ever required of a teacher beyond "readin, writin, and cipherin" to the Rule of Three. If a straggler supposed to understand Latin happen to sojourn in the neighborhood, he was looked upon as a wizard. There was absolutely nothing to excite ambition for education. Of course, when I came of age I did not know much. Still, somehow, I could read, write, and cipher to the rule of three, but that was all. I have not been to school since. The little advance I now have upon this store of education, I have picked up from time to time under the pressure of necessity.

(NH V, 287)

June 1, 1860
In biographical literature he provided for the presidential election
of 1860, Lincoln described his education.

Abraham now thinks that the aggregate of all his schooling did not amount to one year. He was never in a college or academy as a student, and never inside of a college or academy building till he had a law license. What he has in the way of education he has picked up. After he was twenty-three and had separated from his father, he studied English grammar—imperfectly, of course, but so as to speak and write as well as he now does. He studied and nearly mastered the six books of Euclid since he was a member of Congress. He regrets his want of education, and does what he can to supply the want.

(NH VI, 27–28)

August 5, 1863
In a letter to one of his generals, Lincoln suggested that Louisiana's new constitution should include a provision for the education of freed African-Americans.

While I very well know what I would be glad for Louisiana to do, it is quite a different thing for me to assume direction of the matter. I would be glad for her to make a new constitution recognizing the emancipation proclamation, and adopting emancipation in those parts of the state to which the proclamation does not apply. And while she is at it, I think it would not be objectionable for her to adopt some practical system by which the two races could gradually live themselves out of the old relation to each other, and both come out better prepared for the new. Education for young blacks should be included in the plan.

(NH IX, 56–57)

August 17, 1863
Lincoln was very fond of Shakespeare's writings, as he expressed in this letter to actor James H. Hackett.

The first presentation of Falstaff I ever saw was yours here, last winter or spring. Perhaps the best compliment I can pay is to say, as I truly can, I am very anxious to see it again. Some of Shakespeare's plays I have never read; while others I have gone over perhaps as frequently as any unprofessional reader. Among the latter are "Lear," "Richard III," "Henry VIII," "Hamlet," and especially "Macbeth." I think nothing equals "Macbeth." It is wonderful.

Unlike you gentlemen of the profession, I think the soliloquy of "Hamlet" commencing "Oh, my offense is rank," surpasses that commencing "To be or not to be." But pardon this small attempt at criticism.

(NH IX, 85)

December 27, 1864
Letter to the president of the College of New Jersey.

I have the honor to acknowledge the reception of your note of the 20th of December, conveying the announcement that the trustees of the College of New Jersey had conferred upon me the degree of Doctor of Laws. . . . I am most thankful if my labors have seemed to conduct to the preservation of those institutions under which alone we can expect good government—and in its train, sound learning and the progress of the liberal arts.

(NH X, 326–27)

Law

A self-taught lawyer who excelled in the courtroom, Abraham Lincoln distinguished himself as an honest, determined practitioner who carved out a modestly profitable law practice in Illinois, first in partnership with his friend John T. Stuart, then Stephen T. Logan, and finally, his future biographer, William H. Herndon. Traveling the circuit courts improved his political connections, while his time spent arguing cases sharpened his rhetorical skills. Lincoln was frequently approached by young aspiring lawyers who wanted to study under him. His advice to them was based on his own hard-fought experience: "Work, work, work is the main thing."

January 27, 1838
From the Young Men's Lyceum speech, in which Lincoln spoke of lawlessness in various parts of the country. (See Appendix A for complete text.)

When men take it in their heads today to hang gamblers or burn murderers, they should recollect that in the confusion usually attending such transactions they will be likely to hang or burn someone who is neither a gambler nor a murderer as one who is, and that, acting upon the example they set, the mob of tomorrow may, and probably will, hang or burn some of them by the very same mistake. And not only so; the innocent, those who have ever set their faces against violations of law in every shape, alike with the guilty fall victims to the ravages of mob law; and thus it goes up, step by step, till all the walls erected for the defense of the persons and property of individuals are trodden down and disregarded. . . . Having ever regarded government as their deadliest bane, they make a jubilee of the suspension of its operations, and pray for nothing so much as its total annihilation.

(NH I, 40–41)

January 27, 1838
From the Young Men's Lyceum Address.

Let every American, every lover of liberty, every well-wisher to his posterity swear by the blood of the Revolution never to violate in the least particular the laws of the country, and never to tolerate their violation by others. As the patriots of seventy-six did to the support of the Declaration of Independence, so to the support of the Constitution and laws let every American pledge his life, his property, and his sacred honor—let every man remember that to violate the law is to trample on the blood of his father, and to tear the charter of his own and his children's liberty. Let reverence for the laws be breathed by every American mother to the lisping babe that prattles on her lap; let it be taught in schools, in seminaries, and in colleges; let it be written in primers, spelling books, and in almanacs; let it be preached from the pulpit, proclaimed in legislative halls, and enforced in courts of justice. And, in short, let it become the political religion of the nation; and let the old and the young, the rich and the poor, the grave and the gay of all sexes and tongues and colors and conditions, sacrifice unceasingly upon its altars.

(NH I, 42–43)

January 27, 1838
From the Young Men's Lyceum Address.

When I so pressingly urge a strict observance of all the laws, let me not be understood as saying there are no bad laws, or that grievances may not arise for the redress of which no legal provisions have been made. I mean to say no such thing. But I do mean to say that although bad laws, if they exist, should be repealed as soon as possible, still, while they continue in force, for the sake of example they should be religiously observed. So also in unprovided cases. If such arise, let proper legal provisions be made for them with the least possible delay, but till then let them, if not too intolerable, be borne with.

There is no grievance that is a fit object of redress by mob law. In any case that may arise, as, for instance, the promulgation of abolitionism, one of two positions is necessarily true—that is, the thing is right within itself, and therefore deserves the protection of all law and all good citizens, or it is wrong, and therefore proper to be prohibited by legal enactments; and in neither case is the interposition of mob law either necessary, justifiable, or excusable.

(NH I, 44)

February 20, 1848
Legal advice to a friend.

In law, it is good policy to never plead what you need not, lest you oblige yourself to prove what you cannot. Reflect on this well before you proceed.

(NH II, 3)

July 1, 1850
Lincoln's self-effacing description of his own legal abilities, from notes for a law lecture.

I am not an accomplished lawyer. I find quite as much material for a lecture in those points wherein I have failed, as in those wherein I have been moderately successful. The leading rule for the lawyer, as for the man of every other calling, is diligence. Leave nothing for tomorrow which can be done today. Never let your correspondence fall behind. Whatever piece of business you have in hand, before stopping, do all the labor pertaining to it which can then be done.

(CW II, 81)

July 1, 1850
From notes for a law lecture.

Extemporaneous speaking should be practiced and cultivated. It is the lawyer's avenue to the public. However able and faithful he may be in other respects, people are slow to bring him business if he cannot make a speech. And yet there is not a more fatal error to young lawyers than relying too much on speech-making. If any one, upon his rare powers of speaking, shall claim an exemption from the drudgery of the law, his case is a failure in advance.

(CW II, 81)

July 1, 1850
Advice to students considering law as their profession.

Discourage litigation. Persuade your neighbors to compromise whenever you can. Point out to them how the nominal winner is often a real loser—in fees, expenses, and waste of time. As a peacemaker the lawyer has a superior opportunity of being a good man. There will still be business enough.

(CW II, 81)

July 1, 1850
Advice to lawyers.

Never stir up litigation. A worse man can scarcely be found than one who does this. Who can be more nearly a fiend than he who habitually overhauls the register of deeds in search of defects in titles, whereon to stir up strife, and put money in his pocket? A moral tone ought to be infused into the profession which should drive such men out of it.

(CW II, 81–82)

July 1, 1850
Advice to students considering law as their profession.

There is a vague popular belief that lawyers are necessarily dishonest. I say vague, because when we consider to what extent confidence and honors are reposed in and conferred upon lawyers by the people, it appears improbable that their impression of dishonesty is very distinct and vivid. Yet the impression is common, almost universal. Let no young man choosing the law for a calling for a moment yield to the popular belief—resolve to be honest without being a lawyer. Choose some other occupation rather than one in the choosing of which you do, in advance, consent to be a knave.

(NH II, 143)

November 5, 1855
Lincoln received many requests from young men desiring to study law under him.

I am from home too much of my time, for a young man to read law with me advantageously. . . . I did not read with any one. Get the books, and read and study them till you understand them in their principal features; and that is the main thing. . . . Always bear in mind that your own resolution to succeed, is more important than any other one thing.

(CW II, 327)

February 21, 1856
Letter to a client who had asked Lincoln to draw up some legal documents. Lincoln's reputation with clients resulted in his nickname "Honest Abe."

I have just received yours of 16th, with check . . . for twenty-five dollars. You must think I am a high-priced man. You are too liberal with your money.

Fifteen dollars is enough for the job. I send you a receipt for fifteen dollars, and return to you a ten-dollar bill.

(CW II, 332–3)

June 26, 1857
Lincoln on judicial decisions, from a speech on the Dred Scott decision.

Judicial decisions have two uses—first, to absolutely determine the case decided, and secondly, to indicate to the public how other similar cases will be decided when they arise. For the latter use, they are called "precedents" and "authorities" . . . Judicial decisions are of greater or less authority as precedents, according to circumstance. That this should be so, accords both with common sense, and the customary understanding of the legal profession.

(CW II, 400–01)

June 15, 1858
Notes taken during a trial.

Legislation and adjudication must follow and conform to the progress of society. . . . Just reasoning—policy—is in favor of general legislation, else the legislature will be leaded down with the investigation of smaller cases—a work which the courts ought to perform, and can perform much more perfectly.

(NH II, 366–67)

August 3, 1858
Letter to a young man who wanted to study law.

If you wish to be a lawyer, attach no consequence to the place you are in, or the person you are with; but get books, sit down anywhere, and go to reading for yourself. That will make a lawyer of you quicker than any other way.

(CW II, 535)

November 17, 1858
An angry letter sent to a client, regarding the selling of lands involved in a lawsuit.

My mind is made up. I will have no more to do with this class of business. I can do business in court, but I can not, and will not follow executions all over the world. . . . I would not go through the same labor and vexation again for five hundred [dollars]. . . .

(CW III, 338)

August 14, 1860
An opinion regarding the fugitive slave law.

Justice and fairness to all, is the utmost I have said, or will say.

(NH VI, 49)

September 25, 1860
Advice on the best way to study law.

The mode is very simple, though laborious and tedious. It is only to get the books and read and study them carefully. Begin with Blackstone's "Commentaries," and after reading it carefully through, say twice, take up Chitty's "Pleadings," Greenleaf's "Evidence," and Story's "Equity," etc., in succession. Work, work, work, is the main thing.

(NH VI, 59)

December 3, 1861
President Lincoln addressed the problem of Supreme Court vacancies in his annual message to Congress.

I have been unwilling to throw all the appointments northward, thus disabling myself from doing justice to the South on the return of peace; although I may remark that to transfer to the North one which has heretofore been South, would not, with reference to territory and population, be unjust.

(NH VII, 38)

December 3, 1861
In his annual message to Congress, Lincoln spoke about the use collection of Southern debts.

Under these circumstances, I have been urgently solicited to establish, by military power, courts to administer summary justice in such cases. I have thus far declined to do it, not because I had any doubt that the end proposed—the collection of the debts—was just and right itself, but because I have been unwilling to go beyond the pressure of necessity in the unusual exercise of power. But the powers of Congress, I suppose, are equal to the anomalous occasion, and therefore I refer the whole matter to Congress, with the hope that a plan may be devised for the administration of justice . . . whether by a voluntary return to allegiance and order, or by the power of our arms; this, however, not to be a permanent institution, but a temporary substitute, and to cease as soon as the ordinary courts can be reestablished in peace.

(NH VII, 42)

Anecdotes and Stories

Lincoln was a consummate storyteller and often interspersed his political speeches with humorous anecdotes. His folksy jokes and quips, frequently aimed at himself, endeared him to many voters who saw in him an attractive combination of sharp intellect and self deprecating humor.

December 26, 1839
From a speech to the Illinois House of Representatives.

A witty Irish soldier, who was always boasting of his bravery when no danger was near, but who invariably retreated without orders at the first charge of an engagement, being asked by his captain why he did so, replied: "Captain, I have as brave a heart as Julius Caesar ever had; but, somehow or other, whenever danger approaches, my cowardly legs will run away with it."

(NH I, 136–37)

February 22, 1842
An example of how Lincoln used a funny story to illustrate a point, from an address to the Springfield Washington Temperance Society.

What an ignorance of human nature does it exhibit, to ask or expect a whole community to rise up and labor for the temporal happiness of others after themselves shall be consigned to the dust, a majority of which community take no pains whatever to secure their own eternal welfare, at no more distant day? Great distance, in either time or space, has wonderful power to lull and render quiescent the human mind. Pleasures to be enjoyed, or pains to be endured, after we shall be dead and gone are but little regarded even in our own cases, and much less in the cases of others. Still, in addition to this, there is something so ludicrous in promises of good, or threats of evil a great way off, as to render the whole subject with which they are connected, easily to turn into ridicule. "Better lay down that spade you're stealing, Paddy; if you don't you'll pay for it at the day of judgment." "By the powers, if ye'll credit me so long, I'll take another, jist."

(CW I, 275–76)

February 25, 1842
From a letter to Lincoln's friend, Joshua Speed, who had recently married despite having reservations.

My old father used to have a saying that "If you make a bad bargain, hug it the tighter"; and it occurs to me, that if the bargain you have just closed can possibly be called a bad one, it is certainly the most pleasant one for applying that maxim to, which my fancy can, by any effort, picture.

(CW I, 280)

July 27, 1848
An attack on the Democratic Party's dependence on Andrew Jackson, who had been president three terms earlier.

Like a horde of hungry ticks you have stuck to the tail of the Hermitage lion to the end of his life; and you are still sticking to it, and drawing a loathsome sustenance from it, after he is dead. A fellow once advertised that he had made a discovery by which he could make a new man out of an old one, and have enough of the stuff left to make a little yellow dog. Just such a discovery has General Jackson's popularity been to you. You not only twice made president of him out of it, but you have had enough of the stuff left to make presidents of several comparatively small men since; and it is your chief reliance now to make still another.

(NH II, 73)

July 27, 1848
Lincoln sometimes put himself down as an indirect way of ridiculing a political opponent, as he did when comparing his own short military career with that of General Lewis Cass, a Senator campaigning for the Democratic presidential nomination.

By the way Mr. Speaker, did you know I am a military hero? Yes sir; in the days of the Black Hawk war I fought, bled, and came away. Speaking of General Cass's career reminds me of my own. I was not at Stillman's defeat, but I was about as near it as Cass was to Hull's surrender; and, like him, I saw the place very soon afterward. It is quite certain I did not break my sword, for I had none to break; but I bent a musket pretty badly on one occasion. If Cass broke his sword, the idea is he broke it in desperation; I bent the musket by accident. If General Cass went in advance of me in picking huckleberries, I guess I surpassed him in charges upon the wild onions. If he saw any live, fighting Indians, it was more than I did; but I had a good many bloody struggles with the mosquitoes, and although I never fainted from the loss of blood, I can truly say I was often very hungry.

(NH II, 75–76)

July 27, 1848
More of Lincoln's attack on Democratic presidential candidate Lewis Cass.

Mr. Speaker, we have all heard of the animal standing in doubt between two stacks of hay and starving to death. The like of that would never happen to General Cass. Place the stacks a thousand miles apart, he would stand stock-still midway between them, and eat them both at once, and the green grass along the line would be apt to suffer some, too, at the same time. By all means make him president, gentlemen. He will feed you bounteously—if—if there is any left after he shall have helped himself.

(NH II, 83)

July 27, 1848
Lincoln's comment on the divisions within the Democratic Party during the 1848 presidential election.

I have heard of some things from New York; and if they are true, one might well say of your party there, as a drunken fellow once said when he head the reading of an indictment for hog-stealing. The clerk read on till he got to and through the words, "did steal, take, and carry away ten boars, ten sows, ten shoats, and ten pigs," at which time he exclaimed, "Well, by golly, that is the most equally divided gang of hogs I ever did hear of!" If there is any other gang of hogs more equally divided than the Democrats of New York are about this time, I have not heard of it.

(NH II, 88)

February 13, 1856
From a request to R.P. Morgan for a railway pass.

Says Tom to John: "Here's your old rotten wheelbarrow. I've broke it, usin' on it. I wish you would mend it, case I shall want to borrow it this arter-noon."

(NH II, 289)

August 21, 1858
During their first debate, Stephen Douglas characterized Lincoln as a "kind, amiable, and intelligent man," prompting this response.

I was a little "taken," for it came from a great man. I was not very much accustomed to flattery, and it came the sweeter to me. I was rather like the Hoosier with the gingerbread, when he said he reckoned he loved it better than any other man, and got less of it.

(NH III, 238)

October 7, 1858
Lincoln's response to political distortions published in a Demo-
cratic newspaper.

As the fisherman's wife, whose drowned husband was brought
home with his body full of eels, said when she was asked what was
to be done with him, "Take the eels out and set him again," so
Harris and Douglas have shown a disposition to take the eels out
of that stale fraud by which they gained Harris's election, and set
the fraud again more than once.

(NH IV 279–80)

October 15, 1858
From the last debate with Stephen Douglas.

The Bible says somewhere that we are desperately selfish. I think
we would have discovered that fact without the Bible.

(NH V, 54)

October 15, 1858
A metaphor used to describe the problem of ridding the country of
slavery, during the last of the Lincoln-Douglas debate.

You may have a wen or cancer upon your person, and not be able
to cut it out lest you bleed to death; but surely it is no way to cure
it, to engraft it and spread it over your whole body.

(NH V, 61)

February 22, 1859
From a speech before the Springfield Library Association.

The inclination to exchange thoughts with one another is probably an original impulse of our nature. If I be in pain, I wish to let
you know it, and to ask your sympathy and assistance; and my
pleasurable emotions also I wish to communicate to and share
with you. But to carry on such communications, some instrumen-
tality is indispensable. Accordingly speech—articulate sounds rat-
tled off from the tongue—was used by our first parents, and even

by Adam before the creation of Eve. He gave names to the animals while she was still a bone in his side; and he broke out quite
volubly when she first stood before him, the best present of his
Maker.

(NH V, 104)

April 6, 1859
A comment on the way that Democrats and Republicans had
switched their political platforms.

I remember being once much amused at seeing two partially in-
toxicated men engaged in a fight with their great-coats on, which
fight, after a long and rather harmless contest, ended in each having fought himself out of his own coat and into that of the other.
If the two leading parties of this day are really identical with the
two in the days of Jefferson and Adams, they have performed the
same feat as the two drunken men.

(NH V, 125–26)

September 17, 1859
Lincoln often quoted from the Bible, as he did here with Luke
11:23.

The good old maxims of the Bible are applicable, and truly applicable to human affairs, and in this, as in other things, we may
say here that he who is not for us is against us; he who gathereth
not with us scattereth.

(NH V, 234–35)

September 30, 1859
From a speech to the Wisconsin State Agricultural Society.

It is said an Eastern monarch once charged his wise men to invent
him a sentence to be ever in view, and which should be true and
appropriate in all times and situations. They presented him the
words, "And this, too, shall pass away." How much it expresses!
How consoling in the depths of affliction!

(NH V, 255)

March 5, 1860
Comment directed at a senator who opposed a strike among shoe factory workers.

A Democratic Senator gets up in the Senate chamber and pompously announces that "I cannot dawt thot this strike is thresult of the onforchunit wahfar brought aboat boy this sucktional controvussy!" And I am glad to know that there is a system of labor where a laborer can strike if he wants to! I would to God that such a system prevailed all over the world.

(CW IV, 7)

March 6, 1860
From a speech in Hartford, Connecticut, referring to Southern threats of secession.

It reminded him of the man who had a poor, old, lean, bony, spavined horse, with swelled legs. He was asked what he was going to do with such a miserable beast—the poor creature would die. "Do?" said he. "I'm going to fat him up; don't you see that I have got him seal fat as high as the knees?" Well they have got the Union dissolved up to the ankle, but no further!

(NH V, 337)

March 6, 1860
A metaphor for the spread of slavery, often employed by Lincoln.

If I saw a venomous snake crawling in the road, any man would say I might seize the nearest stick and kill it; but if I found that snake in bed with my children, that would be another question. I might hurt the children more than the snake, and it might bite them. Much more, if I found it in bed with my neighbor's children, and I had bound myself by a solemn compact not to meddle with his children under any circumstances, it would become me to let that particular mode of getting rid of the gentleman alone. But if there was a bed newly made up, to which the children were to be taken, and it was proposed to take a batch of young snakes and put them there with them, I take it no man would say there was any question how I ought to decide!

(NH V, 347–48)

March 6, 1860
Lincoln discounted the publicized struggle between the races.

"In the struggle between the white man and the negro," assumes that there is a struggle. . . . There is no such struggle. It is merely an ingenious falsehood to degrade and brutalize the negro. Let each let the other alone, and there is no struggle about it. If it was like two wrecked seamen on a narrow plank, where each must push the other off or drown himself, I would push the negro off— or a white man either; but it is not: the plank is large enough for both. This good earth is plenty broad enough for white man and negro both, and there is no need of either pushing the other off.

(NH V, 352)

November 21, 1860
With the country greatly agitated over the possibility of a civil war, Lincoln remained optimistic that common sense would pre-vail.

By the way, I think very much of the people, as an old friend said he thought of woman. He said when he lost his first wife, who had been a great help to him in his business, he thought he was ruined—that he could never find another to fill her place. At length, however, he married another, who he found did quite as well as the first, and that his opinion now was that any woman would do well who was well done by. So I think of the whole people of this nation—they will ever do well if done well by.

(CW IV, 144)

February 20, 1861
Shortly before he assumed office as president, Lincoln addressed the mayor and council of New York City.

I understand that the ship is made for the carrying and the preservation of the cargo; and so long as the ship is safe with the cargo, it shall not be abandoned. This Union shall never be abandoned, unless the possibility of its existence shall cease to exist without the necessity of throwing passengers and cargo overboard. So long, then, as it is possible that the prosperity and liberties of this people can be preserved within this Union, it shall be my purpose at all times to preserve it.

(NH VI, 150)

December 3, 1861
A story intended to illustrate the logic of having one general, McClellan, in command of the entire Union army.

In a storm at sea no one on board can wish the ship to sink; and yet not infrequently all go down together because too many will direct, and no single mind can be allowed to control.

(NH VII, 56)

April 18, 1864
From a speech at a fair in Baltimore, regarding attitudes toward slavery.

The shepherd drives the wolf from the sheep's throat, for which the sheep thanks the shepherd as his liberator, while the wolf denounces him for the same act, as the destroyer of liberty, especially as the sheep was a black one. Plainly, the sheep and the world are not agreed upon a definition of the word liberty; and precisely the same difference prevails today among us human creatures, even in the North, and all professing to love liberty.

(NH IX, 77–78)

PART II

Civil War

The Road to Fort Sumter

Almost thirty years before the outbreak of the Civil War, Lincoln—among others—feared that the nation would be torn apart from within. "Reason," he hoped, "cold, calculating, unimpassioned reason" was the only thing that could heal the widening rift between North and South. Lincoln's moderate anti-slavery stance during the 1860 presidential election inflamed secession-minded Southerners. A month after his election, South Carolina left the Union, followed in quick succession by a majority of the Southern states. Fort Sumter, a federal installation in Charleston Harbor, South Carolina, became the scene of a tense standoff.

January 27, 1837
While serving a second term in the Illinois legislature, Lincoln gave his famous Young Men's Lyceum speech, in which he hinted at the political problems threatening to tear the nation apart. (See Appendix A for complete text.)

At what point shall we expect the approach of danger? By what means shall we fortify against it? Shall we expect some transatlantic military giant to step the ocean, and crush us at a blow? Never! All the armies of Europe, Asia and Africa combined, with all the treasure of the earth (our own excepted) in their military chest; with a Bonaparte for a commander, could not by force take a drink from the Ohio or make a track on the Blue Ridge in a trial of a thousand years.

At what point, then, is the approach of danger to be expected? I answer, if it ever reach us it must spring up amongst us; it cannot come from abroad. If destruction be our lot we must ourselves be its author and finisher. As a nation of freemen we must live through all time, or die by suicide.

I hope I am over wary; but if I am not, there is even now something of ill omen amongst us. I mean the increasing disregard for law which pervades the country—the growing disposition to substitute the wild and furious passions in lieu of the sober judgment of courts, and the worse than savage mobs for the executive ministers of justice. This disposition is awfully fearful in any community; and that it now exists in ours, though grating to our feelings to admit, it would be a violation of truth and an insult to our intelligence to deny.

(NH I, 37)

January 27, 1837
In his Lyceum speech, Lincoln expressed pessimism about the ability of Americans to preserve the legacy of the Founders.

The experiment is successful, and thousands have won their deathless names in making it so. But the game is caught; and I believe it is true that with the catching end the pleasures of the chase. This field of glory is harvested, and the crop is already appropriated. But new reapers will arise, and they too will seek a field. It is to deny what the history of the world tells us is true, to suppose that men of ambition and talents will not continue to spring up amongst us. And when they do, they will as naturally seek the gratification of their ruling passion as others have done before them. The question is, can that gratification be found in supporting and maintaining an edifice that has been erected by others? Most certainly it cannot.

(NH I, 46)

January 27, 1837
Lincoln predicted that a rogue leader could destroy the nation
from within.

Towering genius disdains a beaten path. It seeks regions hitherto unexplored. It sees no distinction in adding story to story upon the monuments of fame erected to the memory of others. It denies that it is glory enough to serve under any chief. It scorns to tread in the footsteps of any predecessor, however illustrious. It thirsts and burns for distinction; and if possible, will have it, whether at the expense of emancipating slaves or enslaving freemen. Is it unreasonable, then, to expect that some man possessed of the loftiest genius, coupled with ambition sufficient to push it to its utmost stretch, will at some time spring up among us? And when such an one does, it will require the people to be united with each other, attached to the government and laws, and generally intelligent, to successfully frustrate his designs.

(NH I, 46–47)

January 27, 1837
Further in the Lyceum speech, Lincoln despaired over the state of
national feeling.

The jealousy, envy, and avarice incident to our nature, and so common to a state of peace, prosperity, and conscious strength, were for the time in a great measure smothered and rendered inactive, while the deep-rooted principles of hate, and the powerful motive of revenge, instead of being turned against each other, were directed exclusively against the British nation. And thus, from the force of circumstances, the basest principles of our nature were either made to lie dormant, or to become the active agents in the advancement of the noblest of causes—that of establishing and maintaining civil and religious liberty.

But this state of feeling must fade, is fading, has faded, with the circumstances that produced it.

(NH I, 48)

January 27, 1837
Lincoln insisted that reason must prevail if the nation was to be saved.

They were a fortress of strength; but what invading foeman could never do, the silent artillery of time has done—the leveling of its walls. They are gone. They were a forest of giant oaks; but the all-resistless hurricane has swept over them, and left only here and there a lonely trunk, despoiled of its verdure, shorn of its foliage, unshading and unshaded, to murmur in a few more gentle breezes, and to combat with its mutilated limbs a few more ruder storms, then to sink and be no more.

They were pillars of the temple of liberty; and now that they have crumbled away that temple must fall unless we, their descendants, supply their places with other pillars, hewn from the solid quarry of sober reason. Passion has helped us, but can do so no more. It will in future be our enemy. Reason—cold, calculating, unimpassioned reason—must furnish all the materials for our future support and defense. Let those materials be molded into general intelligence, sound morality, and, in particular, a reverence for the Constitution and laws; and that we improved to the last, that we remained free to the last, that we revered his name to the last, that during his long sleep we permitted no hostile foot to pass over or desecrate his resting place, shall be that which to learn the last trump shall awaken our Washington.

Upon these let the proud fabric of freedom rest, as the rock of its basis; and as truly as has been said of the only greater institution, "the gates of hell shall not prevail against it."

(NH I, 49–50)

October 16, 1854
The repeal of the Missouri Compromise was seen by Lincoln as a tremendous blow to the fragile accord that had been in place for thirty-four years.

The spirit of mutual concession—that spirit which first gave us the Constitution, and which has thrice saved the Union—we shall have strangled and cast from us forever. And what shall we have in lieu of it? The South flushed with triumph and tempted to excess; the North, betrayed as they believe, brooding on wrong and burning for revenge. One side will provoke, the other resent. The one will taunt, the other defy; one aggresses, the other retaliates. Already a few in the North defy all constitutional restraints, resist the execution of the fugitive-slave law, and even menace the institution of slavery in the states where it exists. Already a few in the South claim the constitutional right to take and to hold slaves in the free states—demand the revival of the slave trade—and demand a treaty with Great Britain by which fugitive slaves may be reclaimed from Canada. As yet they are but few on either side. It is a grave question for lovers of the Union, whether the final destruction of the Missouri Compromise, and with it the spirit of all compromise, will or will not embolden and embitter each of these, and fatally increase the number of both.

(NH II, 240–41)

October 16, 1854
Near the close of his famous speech in Peoria, Lincoln invoked the language of Thomas Jefferson, who in 1787 stated that "The tree of liberty must be refreshed from time to time with the blood of patriots and tyrants."

Our republican robe is soiled and trailed in the dust. Let us repurify it. Let us turn and wash it white in the spirit, if not the blood, of the Revolution. Let us turn slavery from its claims of "moral right" back upon its existing legal rights and its arguments of "necessity." Let us return it to the position our fathers gave it, and there let it rest in peace. Let us readopt the Declaration of Independence, and with it the practices and policy which harmonize with it. Let North and South—let all Americans—let all lovers of liberty everywhere join in the great and good work. If we do this, we shall not only have saved the Union, but we shall have so saved it as to make and to keep it forever worthy of the saving. We shall have so saved it that the succeeding millions of free, happy people, the world over, shall rise up and call us blessed to the latest generations.

(NH II, 248)

August 24, 1855
Lincoln was appalled by the repeal of the Missouri Compromise.

I look upon that enactment not as a law, but as a violence from the beginning. It was conceived in violence, because the destruction of the Missouri Compromise, under the circumstances, was nothing less than violence. It was passed in violence, because it could not have passed at all but for the votes of many members in violence of the known will of their constituents. It is maintained in violence, because the election since clearly demand its repeal; and the demand is openly disregarded.

(NH II, 283)

August 24, 1855
In a letter to Joshua Speed, Lincoln riled against the Know Nothings, an anti-immigration, anti-Catholic political organization that rose to power in 1854.

Our progress in degeneracy appears to me to be pretty rapid. As a nation we began by declaring that "all men are created equal." We now practically read it "all men are created equal, except negroes." When the Know Nothings get control, it will read "all men are created equal, except negroes and foreigners and Catholics." When it comes to this, I shall prefer emigrating to some country where they make no pretense of loving liberty—to Russia, for instance, where despotism can be taken pure, and without the base alloy of hypocrisy.

(NH II, 287)

August 27, 1856
From a speech in Kalamazoo, Michigan, in which Lincoln countered the charge that the Union was endangered by radical aboli-

tionists within the Republican Party. Lincoln was derided as the "great high priest of abolitionism" and the "depot master of the underground railroad" in an article that appeared several days later in the Illinois State Register.

How is the dissolution of the Union to be consummated? They tell us that the Union is in danger. Who will divide it? Is it those who make the charge? Are they themselves the persons who wish to see this result? A majority will never dissolve the Union. Can a minority do it?

(CW II, 366)

October 1, 1856
Part of a speech on sectionalism.

Recurring to the question, "Shall slavery be allowed to extend into United States territory now legally free?" This is a sectional question—that is to say, it is a question in its nature calculated to divide the American people geographically. Who is to blame for that? Who can help it? Either side can hold it; but how? Simply by yielding to the other side; there is no other way; in the whole range of possibility there is no other way. Then, which side shall yield? To this, again, there can be but one answer—the side which is in the wrong. True, we differ as to which side is wrong, and we boldly say, let all who really think slavery ought to be spread into free territory, openly go over against us; there is where they rightfully belong. But why should any go who really think slavery ought not to spread? Do they really think the right ought to yield to the wrong? Are they afraid to stand by the right? Do they fear that the Constitution is too weak to sustain them in the right? Do they really think that by right surrendering to wrong the hopes of our Constitution, our Union, and our liberties can possibly be bettered?

(NH II, 306–07)

May 18, 1858
From Lincoln's notes for a speech on the pro-slavery Lecompton
Constitution, which, if enacted, would have admitted the Kansas
Territory as a slave state.

Welcome or unwelcome, agreeable or disagreeable, whether this shall be an entire slave nation is the issue before us. Every incident—every little shifting of scenes or of actors—only clears away the intervening trash, compacts and consolidates the opposing hosts, and brings them more and more distinctly face to face. The conflict will be a severe one; and it will be fought through by those who do care for the result, and not those who do not care—by those who are for, and those who are against, a legalized national slavery. The combined charge of Nebraskaism and Dred-Scottism must be repulsed and rolled back. The deceitful cloak of "self-government," wherewith "the sum of all villainies" seeks to protect and adorn itself, must be torn from its hateful carcass. That burlesque upon judicial decisions, and slander and profanation upon the honored names and sacred history of republican America, must be overruled and expunged from the books of authority.

To give the victory to the right, not bloody bullets, but peaceful ballots are necessary. Thanks to our good old Constitution, and organization under it, these alone are necessary. It only needs that every right thinking man, shall go to the polls, and without fear or prejudice, vote as he thinks.

(CW II, 543–44)

June 16, 1858
As a Republican nominee for the U.S. Senate, Lincoln decided to
risk his political future with his famous "House Divided" speech,
delivered in Springfield, Illinois. The "house divided" reference is
from Mark 3:25.

If we could first know where we are, and whither we are tending, we could better judge what to do, and how to do it. We are now far into the fifth year since a policy was initiated with the avowed object and confident promise of putting an end to slavery agitation. Under the operation of that policy, that agitation has not only not ceased, but has been constantly augmented. In my opinion, it will not cease until a crisis shall have been reached and passed. "A house divided against itself cannot stand." I believe this government cannot endure permanently half slave and half free. I do not expect the Union to be dissolved—I do not expect the house to fall—but I do expect it will cease to be divided. It will become all one thing, or all the other. Either the opponents of slavery will arrest the further spread of it, and place it where the public mind shall rest in the belief that it is in the course of ultimate extinction; or its advocates will push it forward till it shall become alike lawful in all the states, old as well as new, North as well as South.

(NH III, 1–2)

June 16, 1858
The closing paragraph of Lincoln's "House Divided" speech.

Our cause, then, must be entrusted to, and conducted by, its own undoubted friends—those whose hands are free, whose hearts are in the work, who do care for the result. Two years ago the Republicans of the nation mustered over thirteen hundred thousand strong. We did this under the single impulse of resistance to a common danger, with every external circumstance against us. Of strange, discordant, and even hostile elements, we gathered from the four winds, and formed and fought the battle through, under the constant hot fire of a disciplined, proud, and pampered enemy. Did we brave all then to falter now?—now, when that same enemy is wavering, dissevered, and belligerent? The result is not doubtful. We shall not fail—if we stand firm, we shall not fail. Wise counsels may accelerate or mistakes delay it, but, sooner or later, the victory is sure to come.

(NH III, 14–15)

September 17, 1859
During a speech in Cincinnati, Ohio, Lincoln challenged seces-
sionists in the audience.

Well, then, I want to know what you are going to do with your half of it? Are you going to split the Ohio down through, and push your half off a piece? Or are you going to keep it right alongside of us outrageous fellows? . . . You have divided the Union because we would not do right with you, as you think, upon that subject; when we cease to be under obligations to do anything for you, how much better do you think you will be? Will you make war upon us and kill us all? Why, gentlemen, I think you are as gallant and as brave men as live; that you can fight as bravely in a good cause, man for man, as any other people living; that you have shown yourselves capable of this upon various occasions; but man for man, you are not better than we are, and there are not so many of you as there are of us. You will never make much of a hand at whipping us. If we were fewer in numbers than you, I think that you could whip us; if we were equal it would likely be a drawn battle; but being inferior in numbers, you will make nothing by attempting to master us.

(NH V, 219–20)

February 27, 1860
Comments directed at Southerners during an address at the Cooper
Institute, New York.

Your purpose then, plainly stated, is that you will destroy the government, unless you be allowed to construe and force the Constitution as you please, on all points in dispute between you and us. You will rule or ruin in all events.

(NH V, 320)

February 27, 1860
During his address at the Cooper Institute, Lincoln called on
members of his party to remain calm during the sectional contro-
versy.

A few words now to Republicans. It is exceedingly desirable that
all parts of this great Confederacy shall be at peace, and in harmony with another. Let us Republicans do our part to have it so.
Even though much provoked, let us do nothing through passion
and ill temper. Even though the Southern people will not so much
as listen to us, let us calmly consider their demands, and yield to
them if, in our deliberate view of our duty, we possibly can.
Judging by all they say and do, and by the subject and nature of
their controversy with us, let us determine, if we can, what will
satisfy them.

(NH V, 323–24)

February 27, 1860
Lincoln's closing comments at the Cooper Institute.

Let us be diverted by none of those sophistical contrivances wherewith we are so industriously plied and belabored—contrivances
such as groping for some middle ground between the right and
the wrong: vain as the search for a man who should be neither a
living man nor a dead man; such as a policy of "don't care" on a
question about which all true men do care; such as Union appeals
beseeching true Union men to yield to Disunionists, reversing the
divine rule, and calling, not the sinners, but the righteous to repentance; such as invocations to Washington, imploring men to
unsay what Washington said and undo what Washington did.

Neither let us be slandered from our duty by false accusations
against us, nor frightened from it by menaces of destruction to the
government, nor of dungeons to ourselves. Let us have faith that
right makes might, and in that faith let us to the end dare to do
our duty as we understand it.

(NH V, 327–28)

March 5, 1860
In Hartford, Connecticut, Lincoln challenged Republicans to take a firm stand against the spread of slavery.

If our sense of duty forbids this extension, let us do that duty. This contrivance of a middle ground is such that he who occupies it is neither a dead or a living man.

(CW IV, 8)

August 15, 1860
During his bid for the presidential nomination, Lincoln continued to express hope that war could be averted.

I receive from the South that in no probable event will there be any very formidable effort to break up the Union. The people of the South have too much of good sense, and good temper, to attempt the ruin of the government, rather than see it administered as it was administered by the men who made it. At least, so I hope and believe.

(CW IV, 95)

October 26, 1860
Shortly before he was elected, Lincoln wrote to Major David Hunter concerning reports that some army officers were planning to defect to the South.

I have another letter, from a writer unknown to me, saying the officers of the army at Fort Kearny have determined, in case of Republican success at the approaching presidential election, to take themselves, and the arms at that point south for the purpose of resistance to the government. While I think there are many chances to one that this is a humbug, it occurs to me that any real movement of this sort in the army would leak out and become known to you. In such case, if it would not be unprofessional or dishonorable (of which you are to be the judge), I shall be much obliged if you will apprise me of it.

(NH VI, 65)

November 16, 1860
In the weeks following his election, Lincoln refused to answer
those who wrote to ask for a clarification of his policies, telling
them instead to read his many published speeches.

I could say nothing which I have not already said, and which is in
print and accessible to the public. . . . I am not at liberty to shift
my ground—that is out of the question. If I thought a repetition
would do any good I would make it. But my judgment is it would
do positive harm. The secessionists, per se believing they had
alarmed me, would clamor all the louder.

(CW IV, 139–40)

November 20, 1860
Part of a speech that Lincoln wrote for Republican Senator
Lyman Trumbull, which was delivered the following day in
Springfield, Illinois.

I am rather glad of this military preparation in the South. It will
enable the people the more easily to suppress any uprisings there,
which their misrepresentations of purposes may have encouraged.

(CW IV, 142)

December 13, 1860
There was great pressure on President-elect Lincoln to appease
the seceded southern states, but he refused to shift his ground, as in
this letter to Congressman Elihu B. Washburne.

Prevent, as far as possible, any of our friends from demoralizing
themselves, and our cause, by entertaining propositions for compromise of any sort, on "slavery extension." There is no possible
compromise upon it, but which puts us under again, and leaves all
our work to do over again. Whether it be a Mo. Line or Eli
Thayer's Pop[ular] Sov[ereignty], it is all the same. Let either be
done, and immediately filibustering and extending slavery recom-
mences. On that point hold firm, as with a chain of steel.

(CW IV, 151)

December 15, 1860
To Representative John A. Gilmer of North Carolina, who wrote
to ask what Lincoln's policies would be once he was inaugurated.

In one word, I never have been, am not now, and probably never shall be, in a mood of harassing the people, either North or South.

(CW IV, 152)

December 21, 1860
Congressman Elihu Washburne transmitted General Winfield
Scott's warning that Charleston's forts—Moultrie and Sumter—
were dangerously undefended against a potential Southern at-
tack.

Please present my respects to the General, and tell him, confidentially, I shall be obliged to him to be as well prepared as he can to either hold or retake the forts, as the case may require, at, and after the inauguration.

(CW IV, 159)

December 22, 1860
Letter to Major David Hunter, two days after the South
Carolina Legislature voted to secede from the Union.

The most we can do now is to watch events, and be as well prepared as possible for any turn things may take. If the forts fall, my judgment is that they are to be retaken.

(NH VI, 86)

December 28, 1860
Lincoln attempted unsuccessfully to convince the Southern states
to remain in the Union.

I declare that the maintenance inviolate of the rights of the states, and especially the right of each state to order and control its own domestic institutions according to its own judgment exclusively, is essential to that balance of powers on which the perfection and

endurance of our political fabric depend; and I denounce the lawless invasion by armed force of the soil of any state or territory, no
matter under what pretext, as the gravest of crimes.

I am greatly averse to writing anything for the public at this
time; and I consent to the publication of this only upon the condition that six of the twelve United States senators for the states
of Georgia, Alabama, Mississippi, Louisiana, Florida, and Texas
shall sign their names to what is written on this sheet below my
name, and allow the whole to be published together.

"We recommend to the people of the states we represent respectively, to suspend all action for dismemberment of the Union,
at least until some act deemed to be violative of our rights shall be
done by the incoming administration."

(NH VI, 88–89)

January 14, 1861
*Letter to General John E. Wool, who secured Virginia's Fort
Monroe for the Union.*

As to how the military force of the government may become necessary to the preservation of the Union, and more particularly
how that force can best be directed to the object, I must chiefly
rely upon General Scott and yourself. It affords me the profoundest satisfaction to know that with both of you judgment and feeling go heartily with your sense of professional and official duty to
the work.

(NH VI, 98)

January 19–21, 1861
*Remarks made to Illinois Representative William Kellogg, as
published in the* New York Herald *and other prominent newspapers.*

I will suffer death before I will consent or will advise my friends to
consent to any concession or compromise which looks like buying
the privilege of taking possession of this government to which we

have a constitutional right; because, whatever I might think of the merit of the various propositions before Congress, I should regard any concession in the face of menace the destruction of the government itself, and a consent on all hands that our system shall be brought down to a level with the existing disorganized state of affairs in Mexico. But this thing will hereafter be as it is now, in the hands of the people; and if they desire to call a Convention to remove any grievances complained of, or to give new guarantees for the permanence of vested rights, it is not mine to oppose.

(CW IV, 175–76)

February 15, 1861
Part of an address to well-wishers in Pittsburgh, Pennsylvania, prior to Lincoln's inauguration.

I repeat, then, there is no crisis, excepting such a one as may be gotten up at any time by turbulent men aided by designing politicians. My advice to them, under such circumstances, is to keep cool. If the great American people only keep their temper on both sides of the line, the troubles will come to an end, and the question which now distracts the country will be settled, just as surely as all other difficulties of a like character which have originated in this government have been adjusted.

(NH VI, 125–26)

February 21, 1861
From an address to the New Jersey Assembly.

The man does not live who is more devoted to peace than I am, none who would do more to preserve it, but it may be necessary to put the foot down firmly.

(NH VI, 154)

February 22, 1861
From an address at Independence Hall, Philadelphia.

The government will not use force, unless force is used against it.

(NH VI, 158)

February 22, 1861
While in Philadelphia, Lincoln was greeted by a thirty-four-gun
salute and gave this reply to a speech by the governor of Penn-
sylvania.

While I have been proud to see today the finest military array, I think, that I have ever seen, allow me to say, in regard to those men, that they give hope of what may be done when war is inevitable. But, at the same time, allow me to express the hope that in the shedding of blood their services may never be needed, especially in the shedding of fraternal blood.

(NH VI, 161)

March 4, 1861
In his first inaugural address, President Lincoln tried to reason
with secession-minded Southerners. (See Appendix C for complete
text.)

Before entering upon so grave a matter as the destruction of our national fabric, with all its benefits, its memories, and its hopes, would it not be wise to ascertain precisely why we do it? Will you hazard so desperate a step while there is any possibility that any portion of the ills you fly from have no real existence? Will you, while the certain ills you fly to are greater than all the real ones you fly from—will you risk the commission of so fearful a mistake?

(NH VI, 177)

March 4, 1861
From the first inaugural address.

Plainly, the central idea of secession is the essence of anarchy. A majority held in restraint by constitutional checks and limitations, and always changing easily with deliberate changes of popular opinions and sentiments, is the only true sovereign of a free people. Whoever rejects it does, of necessity, fly to anarchy or to despotism. Unanimity is impossible; the rule of a minority, as a permanent arrangement, is wholly inadmissible; so that, rejecting the majority principle, anarchy or despotism in some form is all that is left.

(NH VI, 179)

March 4, 1861
Lincoln's closing words in his first inaugural address.

In your hands, my dissatisfied fellow countrymen, and not in mine, is the momentous issue of civil war. The government will not assail you. You can have no conflict without being yourselves the aggressors. You have no oath registered in heaven to destroy the government, while I shall have the most solemn one to "preserve, protect, and defend it." I am loath to close. We are not enemies, but friends. We must not be enemies. Though passion may have strained, it must not break our bonds of affection. The mystic chords of memory, stretching from every battlefield and patriot grave to every living heart and hearthstone all over this broad land, will yet swell the chorus of the Union when again touched, as surely they will be, by the better angels of our nature.

(NH VI, 184–85)

March 15, 1861
Immediately after taking office, Lincoln asked the members of his cabinet for written opinions on how to supply Fort Sumter, which had been cut off from aid for several months.

Assuming it to be possible to now provision Fort Sumter, under all the circumstances is it wise to attempt it?

(NH VI, 192)

April 4, 1861
Instructions to Major Robert Anderson, the commander at Fort Sumter. The letter was blocked from reaching Anderson by Southern troops.

Hoping still that you will be able to sustain yourself till the 11th or 12th [of April,] the expedition will go forward; and, finding your flag flying, will attempt to provision you, and, in case the effort is resisted, will endeavor also to reinforce you.

It is not, however, the intention of the President to subject your command to any danger or hardship beyond what, in your judgment, would be usual in military life; and he has entire confidence that you will act as becomes a patriot and a soldier, under all circumstances.

Whenever, if at all, in your judgment, to save yourself and command, a capitulation becomes a necessity, you are authorized to make it.

(CW IV, 321)

April 6, 1861
Orders from President Lincoln for an expedition to supply the besieged troops at Fort Sumter.

You will proceed directly to Charleston, South Carolina; and if, on your arrival there, the flag of the United States shall be flying over Fort Sumter, and the fort shall not have been attacked, you will procure an interview with Governor Pickens, and read to him as follows: "I am directed by the President of the United States to notify you to expect an attempt will be made to supply Fort Sumter with provisions only; and that, if such attempt be not resisted, no effort to throw in men, arms, or ammunition will be made without further notice, or in case of an attack upon the fort."

(NH VI, 241)

War Between the States

The Southern bombardment of Fort Sumter ignited the Civil War. Initial hopes for a quick federal victory were dashed at the Battle of Bull Run, where Union forces were routed. George McClellan succeeded the aging General Winfield Scott, but McClellan and a succession of other Union generals were unable to gain a decisive victory over the Confederates, despite advantages in manpower and arms. As the war dragged on, President Lincoln assumed unprecedented executive power with his frequent suspension of the writ of habeas corpus and intimate involvement in military matters, including recommendations for troop movements and the revocation of many death sentences for court-martialed soldiers. Not until General Ulysses S. Grant was appointed general-in-chief of the Union army did Lincoln find someone he could trust to prosecute the war to the fullest.

April 13, 1861
During an attempt to provision Fort Sumter on April 12, Confederate batteries opened fire, thus initiating the Civil War. A committee of three delegates from Virginia was at the White House when news of the attack was heard.

But if, as now appears to be true, in pursuit of a purpose to drive the United States authority from these places, an unprovoked assault has been made upon Fort Sumter, I shall hold myself at liberty to repossess, if I can, like places which had been seized before the government was devolved upon me. And in every event I shall, to the extent of my ability, repel force by force.

(NH VI, 244)

April 15, 1861
In response to the attack on Fort Sumter, Lincoln issued a series of proclamations calling up state militias.

Whereas the laws of the United States have been for some time past and now are opposed, and the execution thereof obstructed, in the states of South Carolina, Georgia, Alabama, Florida, Mississippi, Louisiana, and Texas, by combinations too powerful to be suppressed by the ordinary course of judicial proceedings, or by the powers vested in the marshals by law:

Now, therefore, I, Abraham Lincoln, President of the United States, in virtue of the power in me vested by the Constitution and the laws, have thought fit to call forth, and hereby do call forth, the militia of the several states of the Union, to the aggregate number of seventy-five thousand, in order to suppress said combinations, and to cause the laws to be duly executed.

The details for this object will be immediately communicated to the state authorities through the War Department.

I appeal to all loyal citizens to favor, facilitate, and aid this effort to maintain the honor, the integrity, and the existence of our national Union, and the perpetuity of popular government; and to redress wrongs already long enough endured.

(NH VI, 246)

April 19, 1861
A proclamation for the blockading of Southern ports, which was passed by Congress while in special session.

I, Abraham Lincoln . . . have further deemed it advisable to set on foot a blockade of the ports . . . in pursuance of the laws of the United States, and of the law of nations in such case provided. For this purpose a competent force will be posted so as to prevent entrance and exit of vessels from the ports aforesaid. If, therefore, with a view to violate such blockade, a vessel shall approach or shall attempt to leave either of said ports, she will be duly warned by the commander of one of the blockading vessels, who will indorse on her register the fact and date of such warning, and if the same vessel shall again attempt to enter or leave the blockaded port, she will be captured and sent to the nearest convenient port, for such proceedings against her and her cargo, as prize, as may be deemed advisable.

(NH VI, 249–50)

April 20, 1861
News that federal troops would be transported through Maryland, a border state with a pro-Southern government, caused the governor of Maryland and the mayor of Baltimore to request that troops not be allowed into the state. Lincoln tried to assuage the men, knowing that Maryland was critical for the protection of Washington.

Without any military knowledge myself, of course I must leave details to General Scott. He hastily said this morning in the presence of these gentlemen, "March them around Baltimore, and not through it." I sincerely hope the general, on fuller reflection, will consider this practical and proper, and that you will not object to it. By this a collision of the people of Baltimore with the troops will be avoided, unless they go out of their way to seek it. I hope you will exert your influence to prevent this.

(NH VI, 251)

April 24, 1861
Lincoln was criticized by some in the North for moving federal troops to protect the government in Washington.

I do say the sole purpose of bringing troops here is to defend this capital. I do say I have no purpose to invade Virginia with them or any other troops, as I understand the word invasion. But, suppose Virginia sends her troops, or admits others through her borders, to assail this capital, am I not to repel them even to the crossing of the Potomac, if I can? Suppose Virginia erects, or permits to be erected, batteries on the opposite shore to bombard the city, are we to stand still and see it done? In a word, if Virginia strikes us, are we not to strike back, and as effectively as we can?

(NH VI, 255)

April 25, 1861
Faced with a Maryland Legislature that might vote for secession, Lincoln ordered General Winfield Scott to stand by with federal troops. Maryland was essential for the protection of Washington.

I therefore conclude that it is only left to the commanding general to watch and wait their action, which, if it shall be to arm their people against the United States, he is to adopt the most prompt and efficient means to counteract, even, if necessary, to the bombardment of their cities, and, in the extremest necessity, the suspension of the writ of habeas corpus.

(NH VI, 256)

July 4, 1861
In a special session of Congress, Lincoln speculated on the larger meaning of the conflict between North and South.

This issue embraces more than the fate of these United States. It presents to the whole family of man the question whether a constitutional republic or democracy—a government of the people by the people—can or cannot maintain its territorial integrity against its own domestic foes. It presents the question whether discontented individuals, too few in numbers to control administration according to organic law in any case, can always, upon the pretenses made in this case, or on any other pretenses, or arbitrarily without any pretense, break up their government, and thus practically put an end to free government upon the earth. It forces us to ask: "Is there, in all republics, this inherent and fatal weakness?" "Must a government, of necessity, be too strong for the liberties of its own people, or too weak to maintain its own existence?"

(NH VI, 304)

July 4, 1861
During the special session of Congress, Lincoln stressed the importance of the Border States lying between the North and the newly formed Confederate States.

In the border states, so called, in fact, the Middle States, there are those who favor a policy which they call "armed neutrality"; that is, an arming of those states to prevent the Union forces passing one way, or the disunion the other, over their soil. This would be disunion completely. Figuratively speaking, it would be the building of an impassable wall along the line of separation—and yet not quite an impassable one, for under the guise of neutrality it would tie the hands of Union men and freely pass supplies from among them to the insurrectionists, which it could not do as an open enemy. At a stroke it would take all the trouble off the hands of secession, except only what proceeds from the external blockade. It would do for the disunionists that which, of all things, they most desire—feed them well, and give them disunion without a struggle of their own. It recognizes no fidelity to the Constitution, no obligation to maintain the Union; and while very many who have favored it are doubtless loyal citizens, it is, nevertheless, very injurious in effect.

(NH VI, 307–08)

July 4, 1861
President Lincoln's rationale for suspending the writ of habeas corpus, as explained to Congress.

The provision of the Constitution that "the privilege of the writ of habeas corpus shall not be suspended, unless when, in cases of rebellion or invasion, the public safety may require it," is equivalent

to a provision—is a provision—that such privilege may be suspended when, in case of rebellion or invasion, the public safety
does require it. It was decided that we have a case of rebellion, and
that the public safety does require the qualified suspension of the
privilege of the writ which was authorized to be made. Now it is
insisted that Congress, and not the Executive, is vested with this
power. But the Constitution itself is silent as to which or who is to
exercise the power; and as the provision was plainly made for a
dangerous emergency, it cannot be believed the framers of the instrument intended that in every case the danger should run its
course until Congress could be called together, the very assem-
bling of which might be prevented, as was intended in this case,
by the rebellion.

(NH VI, 310)

July 4, 1861
Lincoln expressed optimism that the war could be won quickly.

It is now recommended that you give the legal means for making
this contest a short and decisive one: that you place at the control
of the government for the work at least four hundred thousand
men and $400,000,000. That number of men is about one tenth
of those of proper ages within the regions where, apparently, all
are willing to engage; and the sum is less than a twenty-third of
the money value owned by the men who seem ready to devote the
whole.

(NH VI, 311)

July 4, 1861
*Near the close of his address, Lincoln challenged the assembled
Congressmen to provide their full support to the war.*

As a private citizen the executive could not have consented that
these institutions shall perish; much less could he, in betrayal of so
vast and so sacred a trust as the free people have confided to him.
He felt that he had no moral right to shrink, nor even to count the

chances of his own life in what might follow. In full view of his great responsibility he has, so far, done what he has deemed his duty. You will now, according to your own judgment, perform yours.

(NH VI, 324)

August 12, 1861
Four months into the Civil War, President Lincoln called for a national day of fasting.

And whereas when our own beloved country, once, by the blessing of God, united, prosperous, and happy, is now afflicted with faction and civil war, it is peculiarly fit for us to recognize the hand of God in this terrible visitation, and in sorrowful remembrance of our own faults and crimes as a nation and as individuals, to humble ourselves before him and to pray for his mercy—to pray that we may be spared further punishment, though most justly deserved; that our arms may be blessed and made effectual for the reestablishment of law, order, and peace throughout the wide extent of our country; and that the inestimable boon of civil and religious liberty, earned under his guidance and blessing by the labors and sufferings of our fathers, may be restored in all its original excellence:

Therefore, I, Abraham Lincoln, President of the United States, do appoint the last Thursday in September next as a day of humiliation, prayer, and fasting for all the people of the nation. And I do earnestly recommend to all the people, and especially to all ministers and teachers of religion, of all denominations, and to all heads of families, to observe and keep that day, according to their several creeds and modes of worship, in all humility and with all religious solemnity, to the end that the united prayer of the nation may ascend to the Throne of Grace, and bring down plentiful blessings upon our country.

(NH VI, 342–43)

October 1, 1861
As he became more directly involved in directing the war, Lincoln
was often criticized for being slow to supply federal troops, arms
and supplies. Governor Morton of Indiana complained that can-
non and troops were essential to protect nearby Kentucky, a vital
border state.

As to Kentucky, you do not estimate that state as more important
than I do, but I am compelled to watch all points. While I write
this I am, if not in range, at least in hearing of cannon-shot from
an army of enemies more than 100,000 strong. I do not expect
them to capture this city; but I know they would if I were to send
the men and arms from here to defend Louisville, of which there
is not a single hostile armed soldier within forty miles, nor any
force known to be moving upon them from any distance. It is true
the army in our front may make a half-circle around southward
and move on Louisville, but when they do we will make a half-
circle around northward and meet them; and in the meantime we
will get up what forces we can from other sources to also meet
them.

(NH VII, 2)

November 1, 1861
The Battle of Bull Run, the first major engagement of the Civil
War, resulted in a catastrophic defeat for Northern forces. General
Winfield Scott stepped down under criticism that he had rushed
his troops into battle unprepared, and Lincoln appointed the bril-
liant young General George B. McClellan in his place.

The American people will hear with sadness and deep emotion
that General Scott has withdrawn from the active control of the
army, while the President and a unanimous cabinet express their
own and the nation's sympathy in his personal affliction, and their
profound sense of the important public services rendered by him
to his country during his long and brilliant career, among which
will ever be gratefully distinguished his faithful devotion to the

Constitution, the Union, and the flag when assailed by parricidal rebellion. . . . The President is pleased to direct that Major General George B. McClellan assume the command of the army of the United States. The headquarters of the army will be established in the city of Washington.

(NH VII, 14)

November 10, 1861
In a letter to one of his generals, Lincoln tried to explain the chronic shortage of arms.

Be assured we do not forget or neglect you. Much, very much, goes undone; but it is because we have not the power to do it faster than we do. Some of your forces are without arms, but the same is true here and at every other place where we have considerable bodies of troops. The plain matter of fact is, our good people have rushed to the rescue of the government faster than the government can find arms to put into their hands. It would be agreeable to each division of the army to know its own precise destination; but the government cannot immediately, nor inflexibly at any time, determine as to all; nor, if determined, can it tell its friends without at the same time telling its enemies.

(NH VII, 19)

December 3, 1861
President Lincoln described the war's effect on foreign relations in his annual message to Congress.

A disloyal portion of the American people have, during the whole year, been engaged in an attempt to divide and destroy the Union. A nation which endures factious domestic division is exposed to disrespect abroad; and one party, if not both, is sure, sooner or later, to invoke foreign intervention. Nations thus tempted to interfere are not always able to resist the counsels of seeming expediency and ungenerous ambition, although measures adopted under such influences seldom fail to be unfortunate and injurious to those adopting them. . . . The principal lever relied on by the insurgents for exciting foreign nations to hostility against us, as already intimated, is the embarrassment of commerce. Those nations, however, not improbably saw from the first that it was the Union which made as well our foreign as our domestic commerce. They can scarcely have failed to perceive that the effort for disunion produces the existing difficulty; and that one strong nation promises more durable peace and a more extensive, valuable, and reliable commerce than can the same nation broken in hostile fragments.

(NH VII, 28–30)

December 3, 1861
On the boundaries of Washington, D.C., from the annual message to Congress.

The present insurrection shows, I think, that the extension of this District across the Potomac River, at the time of establishing the capital here, was eminently wise, and consequently that the relinquishment of that portion of it which lies within the State of Virginia was unwise and dangerous. I submit for your consideration the expediency of regaining that part of the District and the restoration of the original boundaries thereof, through negotiations with the State of Virginia.

(NH VII, 44)

December 3, 1861
In his annual message to Congress, President Lincoln reported that some Native American tribes had joined the Confederate cause.

Although the government has no official information upon this subject, letters have been written to the Commissioner of Indian Affairs by several prominent chiefs, giving assurance of their loyalty to the United States, and expressing a wish for the presence of federal troops to protect them. It is believed that upon the repossession of the country by the federal forces the Indians will readily cease all hostile demonstrations and resume their former relations to the government.

(NH VII, 46)

December 3, 1861
From the annual message to Congress.

The war continues. In considering the policy to be adopted for suppressing the insurrection, I have been anxious and careful that the inevitable conflict for this purpose shall not degenerate into a violent and remorseless revolutionary struggle.

(NH VII, 51)

December 3, 1861
From the annual message to Congress.

The Union must be preserved; and hence all indispensable means must be employed. We should not be in haste to determine that radical and extreme measures, which may reach the loyal as well as the disloyal, are indispensable.

(NH VII, 52)

December 3, 1861
A history of the first eight months of the Civil War, from the annual message to Congress.

The last ray of hope for preserving the Union peaceably expired at the assault upon Fort Sumter; and a general review of what has occurred since may not be unprofitable. What was painfully uncertain then is much better defined and more distinct now; and the progress of events is plainly in the right direction. The insurgents confidently claimed a strong support from north of Mason and Dixon's line; and the friends of the Union were not free from apprehension of the point. This, however, was soon settled definitely, and on the right side. South of the line, noble little Delaware led off right from the first. Maryland was made to seem against the Union. Our soldiers were assaulted, bridges were burned, and railroads torn up within her limits, and we were many days, at one time, without the ability to bring a single regiment over her soil to the capital. Now her bridges and railroads are repaired and open to the government; she already gives seven regiments to the cause of the Union and none to the enemy; and her people at a regular election, have sustained the Union by a larger majority and a larger aggregate vote than they ever before gave to any candidate or any question. Kentucky, too, for some time in doubt, is now decidedly, and, I think, unchangeably, ranged on the side of the Union. Missouri is comparatively quiet, and, I believe, cannot again be overrun by the insurrectionists.

These three states of Maryland, Kentucky, and Missouri, neither of which would promise a single soldier at first, have now an aggregate of not less than forty thousand in the field for the Union, while of their citizens certainly not more than a third of that number, and they of doubtful whereabouts and doubtful existence, are in arms against it. After a somewhat bloody struggle of months, winter closes on the Union people of western Virginia, leaving them masters of their own country.

An insurgent force of about 1500, for months dominating the narrow peninsular region constituting the counties of Accomac and Northampton, and known as the eastern shore of Virginia, together with some contiguous parts of Maryland, have laid down their arms, and the people there have renewed their allegiance to and accepted the protection of the old flag. This leaves no armed insurrectionist north of the Potomac or east of the Chesapeake.

Also we have obtained a footing at each of the isolated points, on the southern coast, of Hatteras, Port Royal, Tybee Island, near Savannah, and Ship Island; and likewise have some general accounts of popular movements in behalf of the Union in North Carolina and Tennessee.

These things demonstrate that the cause of the Union is advancing steadily and certainly southward.

(NH VII, 52–54)

December 3, 1861
President Lincoln described the South's government in his annual
message to Congress.

It continues to develop that the insurrection is largely, if not exclusively, a war upon the first principle of popular government—
the rights of the people. Conclusive evidence of this is found in
the most grave and maturely considered public documents as well
as in the general tone of the insurgents. In those documents we
find the abridgment of the existing right of suffrage and the de-
nial to the people of all right to participate in the selection of public officers except the legislative, boldly advocated, with labored
arguments to prove that large control of the people in government
is the source of all political evil. Monarchy itself is sometimes
hinted at as a possible refuge from the power of the people.

In my present position I could scarcely be justified were I to
omit raising a warning voice against this approach of returning
despotism.

(NH VII, 56)

April 9, 1862
General McClelland was so hesitant to send his men into battle
that President Lincoln grew impatient.

I suppose the whole force which has gone forward to you is with
you by this time; and if so, I think it is the precise time for you to
strike a blow. By delay the enemy will relatively gain upon you—
that is, he will gain faster by fortifications and reinforcements
than you can by reinforcements alone.

(NH VII, 143)

June 15, 1862
Lincoln also had problems with General Frémont, who likewise
resisted engaging enemy troops and complained about the lack of
sufficient troops.

We have no indefinite power of sending reinforcements; so that
we are compelled rather to consider the proper disposal of the

forces we have than of those we could with to have. We may be able to send you some dribs by degrees, but I do not believe we can do more. As you alone beat Jackson last Sunday, I argue that you are stronger than he is today, unless he has been reinforced; and that he cannot have been materially reinforced, because such reinforcement could only have come from Richmond, and he is much more likely to go to Richmond than Richmond is to come to him. Neither is very likely.

(NH VII, 222)

June 26, 1862
Another letter to General Frémont, regarding a frantic dispatch that contained an inflated estimate of Confederate forces.

The later one of 6:15 P.M., suggesting the probability of your being overwhelmed by 200,000, and talking of where the responsibility will belong, pains me very much. I give you all I can, and act on the presumption that you will do the best you can with what you have, while you continue, ungenerously I think, to assume that I could give you more if I would. I have omitted and shall omit no opportunity to send you reinforcements whenever I possibly can.

(NH VII, 235)

July 1, 1862
With General McClelland engaged in a pitched battle near Richmond, Virginia, Lincoln wrote Secretary of State Seward, suggesting that one hundred thousand additional troops be raised in order to bring a quick end to the war. His estimate tripled by the time the state governors in the North issued their call for volunteers.

Fully concurring in the wisdom of the views expressed to me in so patriotic a manner by you, in the communication of the twenty-eighth day of June, I have decided to call into the service an additional force of 300,000 men. . . . I trust that they may be enrolled without delay, so as to bring this unnecessary and injurious civil war to a speedy and satisfactory conclusion. An order fixing the quotas of the respective states will be issued by the War Department tomorrow.

(NH VII, 241)

July 2, 1862
President Lincoln's response to General McClelland's demand for 50,000 troops to aid in a planned assault on Richmond.

Your dispatch of Tuesday morning induces me to hope your army is having some rest. In this hope allow me to reason with you a moment. When you ask for 50,000 men to be promptly sent you, you surely labor under some gross mistake of fact. . . . I have not, outside of your army, 75,000 men east of the mountains. Thus the idea of sending you 50,000, or any other considerable force, promptly, is simply absurd. If, in your frequent mention of responsibility, you have the impression that I blame you for not doing more than you can, please be relieved of such impression. I only beg that in like manner you will not ask impossibilities of me.

(NH VII, 254–55)

July 3, 1862
Many state governors balked at Lincoln's call for additional troops.

I should not want the half of 300,000 new troops if I could have them now. If I had 50,000 additional troops here now, I believe I could substantially close the war in two weeks. But time is everything, and if I get 50,000 new men in a month, I shall have lost 20,000 old ones during the same month, having gained only 30,000, with the difference between old and new troops still against me. The quicker you send, the fewer you will have to send. Time is everything.

(NH VII, 256–57)

July 26, 1862
In a letter to a Union supporter from Maryland, Lincoln showed
his determination to win the war.

I am a patient man—always willing to forgive on the Christian terms of repentance, and also to give ample time for repentance. Still, I must save this government, if possible. What I cannot do, of course I will not; but it may as well be understood, once for all, that I shall not surrender this game leaving any available card unplayed.

(NH VII, 293–94)

July 28, 1862
In a letter to a supporter in Louisiana, President Lincoln explained the logic of employing slaves who crossed over Union lines.

It is a military necessity to have men and money; and we can get neither in sufficient numbers or amounts if we keep from or drive from our lines slaves coming to them.

(NH VII, 295)

July 28, 1862
Despite his desire to bring the war to a quick end, Lincoln was also determined to act fairly.

I shall not do more than I can, and I shall do all I can, to save the government, which is my sworn duty as well as my personal inclination. I shall do nothing in malice. What I deal with is too vast for malicious dealing.

(NH VII, 298)

July 31, 1862
As the war dragged on, Lincoln grew impatient with accusations that his policies were indecisive.

Broken eggs cannot be mended: but Louisiana has nothing to do now but to take her place in the Union as it was, barring the already broken eggs. The sooner she does, the smaller will be the amount of that which will be past mending. This government cannot much longer play a game in which it stakes all, and its enemies stake nothing. Those enemies must understand that they cannot experiment for ten years trying to destroy the government, and if they fail still come back into the Union unhurt.

(NH VII, 299–300)

August 4, 1862
To the Swiss author Count de Gasparin, regarding the difficulties faced by Northern forces.

You ask, "Why is it that the North with her great armies so often is found with inferiority of numbers face to face with the armies of the South?" While I painfully know the fact, a military man—which I am not—would better answer the question. The fact, I know, has not been overlooked; and I suppose the cause of its continuance lies mainly in the other facts that the enemy holds the interior and we the exterior lines; and that we operate where the people convey information to the enemy, while he operates where they convey none to us. . . . You are quite right as to the importance to us, for its bearing upon Europe, that we should achieve military successes, and the same is true for us at home as well as abroad. Yet it seems unreasonable that a series of successes, extending through half a year, and clearing more than 100,000 square miles of country, should help us so little, while a single half defeat should hurt us so much. But let us be patient.

I am very happy to know that my course has not conflicted with your judgment of propriety and policy. I can only say that I have acted upon my best convictions, without selfishness or malice, and that by the help of God I shall continue to do so.

(NH VII, 302–03)

September 13, 1862
President Lincoln was accused in some newspapers of not doing
enough about Confederate mistreatment of captured African-
American troops.

I am told that whenever the rebels take any black prisoners, free or
slave, they immediately auction them off. . . . For instance, when,
after the late battles at and near Bull Run, an expedition went out
from Washington under a flag of truce to bury the dead and bring
in the wounded, and the rebels seized the blacks who went along
to help, and sent them into slavery, Horace Greeley said in his
paper that the government would probably do nothing about it.
What could I do?

(NH VIII, 31)

September 30, 1862
Though he did not attend a church, President Lincoln was never-
theless a religious man, and frequently contemplated God's will in
the great contest between North and South.

The will of God prevails. In great contests, each party claims to
act in accordance with the will of God. Both may be, and one
must be, wrong. God cannot be for and against the same thing at
the same time. In the present civil war it is quite possible that
God's purpose is something different from the purpose of either
party; and yet the human instrumentalities, working just as they
do, are of the best adaptation to effect his purpose. I am almost
ready to say that this is probably true; that God wills this contest,
and wills that it shall not end yet. By his mere great power on the
minds of the now contestants, he could have either saved or destroyed the Union without a human contest. Yet the contest
began. And, having begun, he could give the final victory to either
side any day. Yet the contest proceeds.

(NH VIII, 52–53)

October 13, 1862
In early October, General McClellan was ordered to move the
Army of the Potomac and attack the enemy, but once again,
McClellan refused, claiming that his troops were ill prepared.

You remember my speaking to you of what I called your over-cautiousness. Are you not over-cautious when you assume that you cannot do what the enemy is constantly doing? Should you not claim to be at least his equal in prowess, and act upon the claim? . . . It is all easy if our troops march as well as the enemy, and it is unmanly to say they cannot do it.

(NH VIII, 57–61)

November 5, 1862
McClellan's inaction resulted in his dismissal by Lincoln. He was
replaced by General Ambrose Burnside.

By direction of the President, it is ordered that Major-General McClellan be relieved from the command of the Army of the Potomac, and that Major-General Burnside take the command of that army.

(NH VIII, 72)

November 24, 1862
Reply to General Carl Schurz, who suggested that Lincoln had
not done enough to ensure a Northern victory in the war.

I have just received and read your letter of the 20th. The purport of it is that we lost the late elections and the administration is failing because the war is unsuccessful, and that I must not flatter myself that I am not justly to blame for it. I certainly know that if the war fails, the administration fails, and that I will be blamed for it, whether I deserve it or not. And I ought to be blamed if I could do better. You think I could do better; therefore you blame me already. I think I could not do better; therefore I blame you for blaming me. . . . I certainly have been dissatisfied with the slowness of Buell and McClellan; but before I relieved them I had great fears I should not find successors to them who would do better; and I am sorry to add that I have seen little since to relieve those fears.

(NH VIII, 84–85)

December 1, 1862
President Lincoln described the state of foreign relations in his annual message to Congress.

The civil war, which has so radically changed, for the moment, the occupations and habits of the American people, has necessarily disturbed the American people, has necessarily disturbed the social condition, and affected very deeply the prosperity of the nations with which we have carried on a commerce that has been steadily increasing throughout a period of half a century. It has, at the same time, excited political ambitions and apprehensions which have produced a profound agitation throughout the civilized world. In this unusual agitation we have forborne from taking part in any controversy between foreign states, and between parties or factions in such states. We have attempted no propagandism, and acknowledged no revolution. But we have left to every nation the exclusive conduct and management of its own affairs.

(NH VIII, 94)

December 1, 1862
Native American tribes became involved in the conflict, as explained in the annual message to Congress.

The Indian tribes upon our frontiers have, during the past year, manifested a spirit of insubordination, and at several points have engaged in open hostilities against the white settlements in their vicinity. The tribes occupying the Indian country south of Kansas renounced their allegiance to the United States, and entered into treaties with the insurgents. Those who remained loyal to the United States were driven from the country. The chief of the Cherokees has visited this city for the purpose of restoring the former relations of the tribe with the United States. He alleges that they were constrained by superior force to enter into treaties with the insurgents, and that the United States neglected to furnish the protection which their treaty stipulations required.

(NH VIII, 107)

December 1, 1862
In his closing remarks to Congress, President Lincoln explained his rationale for issuing the Emancipation Proclamation, which would go into force on January 1, 1863.

Fellow citizens, we cannot escape history. We of this Congress and this administration will be remembered in spite of ourselves. No personal significance or insignificance can spare one or another of us. The fiery trial through which we pass will light us down, in honor or dishonor, to the latest generation. We say we are for the Union. The world will not forget that we say this. We know how to save the Union. The world knows we do know how to save it. We—even we here—hold the power and bear the responsibility. In giving freedom to the slave, we assure freedom to the free—honorable alike in what we give and what we preserve. We shall nobly save or meanly lose the last, best hope of earth. Other means may succeed; this could fail. The way is plain, peaceful, generous, just—a way which, if followed, the world will forever applaud, and God must forever bless.

(NH VIII, 131)

December 22, 1862
Despite a severe defeat of the Army of the Potomac at Fredericksburg, Lincoln continued to support General Burnside.

Although you were not successful, the attempt was not an error, nor the failure other than accident. The courage with which you, in an open field, maintained the contest against an entrenched foe, and the consummate skill and success with which you crossed and recrossed the river in the face of the enemy, show that you possess all the qualities of a great army, which will yet give victory to the cause of the country and of popular government.

(NH VIII, 149–50)

December 23, 1862
From a letter to a young girl whose father was killed in battle three weeks earlier.

In this sad world of ours sorrow comes to all, and to the young it comes with bittered agony because it takes them unawares. The older have learned ever to expect it. I am anxious to afford some alleviation of your present distress. Perfect relief is not possible, except with time. You cannot now realize that you will ever feel better. Is not this so? And yet it is a mistake. You are sure to be happy again. To know this, which is certainly true, will make you some less miserable now. I have had experience enough to know what I say, and you need only to believe it to feel better at once. The memory of your dear father, instead of agony, will yet be a sad, sweet feeling in your heart, of a purer and holier sort than you have known before.

(NH VIII, 152–53)

December 31, 1862
President Lincoln weighed in on the application for statehood by West Virginia, which divided itself from Virginia in order to side with the Union.

We can scarcely dispense with the aid of West Virginia in this struggle; much less can we afford to have her against us, in Congress and in the field. Her brave and good men regard her admission into the Union as a matter of life and death. They have been true to the Union under very severe trials. We have so acted to justify their hopes, and we cannot fully retain their confidence and cooperation if we seem to break faith with them. . . . The division of a state is dreaded as a precedent. But a measure made expedient by a war is no precedent for times of peace.

(NH VIII, 159)

January 5, 1863
Lincoln on God's will.

No one is more deeply than myself aware that without His favor our highest wisdom is but as foolishness and that our most strenuous efforts would avail nothing in the shadow of His displeasure. I am conscious of no desire for my country's welfare that is not in consonance with His will, and of no plan upon which we may not ask His blessing. It seems to me that if there be one subject upon which all good men may unitedly agree, it is imploring the gracious favor of the God of Nations upon the struggles our people are making for the preservation of their precious birthright of civil and religious liberty.

(NH VIII, 174)

January 26, 1863
When General Ambrose Burnside was unable to secure significant victories against the Confederate army, Lincoln replaced him with General Joseph Hooker. However, Lincoln had serious misgivings about his new appointee.

I have placed you at the head of the Army of the Potomac. Of course I have done this upon what appear to me to be sufficient reasons, and yet I think it best for you to know that there are some things in regard to which I am not quite satisfied with you. I believe you to be a brave and skilful soldier, which of course I like. I also believe you do not mix politics with your profession, in which you are right. You have confidence in yourself, which is a valuable if not an indispensable quality. You are ambitious, which, within reasonable bounds, does good rather than harm; but I think that during General Burnside's command of the army you have taken counsel of your ambition and thwarted him as much as you could, in which you did a great wrong to the country and to a most meritorious and honorable brother officer. I have heard, in such a way as to believe it, of your recently saying that both the army and the government needed a dictator. Of course it was not for this, but in spite of it, that I have given you the command. Only those generals who gain successes can set up dictators. What I now ask of you is military success, and I will risk the dictatorship.

(NH VIII, 206–07)

February 22, 1863
In a letter to Reverend Alexander Reed, Lincoln politely declined to address a meeting of the Christian Commission.

Whatever shall be sincerely, and in God's name, devised for the good of the soldier and seaman in their hard spheres of duty, can scarcely fail to be blest. And whatever shall tend to turn our thoughts from the unreasoning and uncharitable passions, prejudices, and jealousies incident to a great national trouble such as ours, and to fix them upon the vast and long-enduring consequences, for weal or for woe, which are to result from the struggle, and especially to strengthen our reliance on the Supreme Being for the final triumph of the right, cannot but be well for us all.

(NH VIII, 217–18)

March 10, 1863
The loss of troops by desertion led President Lincoln to issue an amnesty proclamation.

And whereas, evil-disposed and disloyal persons at sundry places have enticed and procured soldiers to desert and absent themselves from their regiments, thereby weakening the strength of the armies and prolonging the war, giving aid and comfort to the enemy, and cruelly exposing the gallant and faithful soldiers remaining in the ranks to increased hardships and danger: I do therefore call upon all patriotic and faithful citizens to oppose and resist the aforementioned dangerous and treasonable crimes, and to aid in restoring to their regiments all soldiers absent without leave, and to assist in the execution of the act of Congress "for enrolling and calling out the national forces, and for other purposes," and to support the proper authorities in the prosecution and punishment of offenders against said act, and in suppressing the insurrection and rebellion.

(NH VIII, 225)

March 26, 1863
In a letter to Governor Andrew Johnson, Lincoln explained the logic of establishing the U.S. Colored Troops.

The colored population is the great available and yet unavailed force for restoring the Union. The bare sight of fifty thousand armed and drilled black soldiers upon the banks of the Mississippi would end the rebellion at once; and who doubts that we can present that sight if we but take hold in earnest.

(NH VIII, 233)

April 1, 1863
The Confederates were particularly harsh in their treatment of black troops.

I am glad to see the accounts of your colored force at Jacksonville, Florida. I see the enemy are driving at them fiercely, as is to be expected. It is important to the enemy that such a force shall not take shape and grow and thrive in the South, and in precisely the same proportion it is important to us that it shall.

(NH VIII, 239)

May 8, 1863
In order to reinforce dwindling enlistment numbers, Lincoln instated a draft that was later reinforced by the Proclamation Concerning Aliens. The proclamation led to draft riots among New York's immigrant population.

Whereas . . . it was enacted by the said statute that all able-bodied male citizens of the United States, and persons of foreign birth who shall have declared on oath their intention to become citizens under and in pursuance of the laws thereof, between the ages of twenty and forty-five years (with certain exceptions not necessary to be here mentioned), are declared to constitute the national forces, and shall be liable to perform military duty in the service of the United States when called out by the President for that purpose . . . I do hereby order and proclaim that no plea of alienage will be received or allowed to exempt from the obligations imposed by the aforesaid act of Congress, any person of foreign birth who shall have declared on oath his intention to become a citizen of the United States.

(NH VIII, 267–68)

June 12, 1863
In May, Ohio Congressman Clement Vallandingham, an outspoken opponent of the war, was arrested and tried in military court for treason. Lincoln was criticized by many in the North, but he defended his actions in a letter to a group that had written resolutions challenging the constitutionality of his decision.

The resolutions promise to support me in every constitutional measure to suppress the rebellion; and I have not knowingly employed, nor shall knowingly employ, any other. But the meeting, by their resolutions, assert and argue that certain military arrests and proceedings following them, for which I am ultimately responsible are unconstitutional. I think they are not. . . . He who dissuades one man from volunteering, or induces one soldier to desert, weakens the Union cause as much as he who kills a Union soldier in battle. Yet this dissuasion or inducement may be so conducted as to be no defined crime of which any civil court would take cognizance. . . . Must I shoot a simple-minded soldier boy who deserts, while I must not touch a hair of a wily agitator who induces him to desert?

(NH VIII, 299–308)

June 29, 1863
Letter to Congressman William Kellogg, who requested permission to trade cotton in Arkansas.

Few things are so troublesome to the government as the fierceness with which the profits of trading are sought. The temptation is so great that nearly everybody wishes to be in it; and, when in, the question of profit controls all, regardless of whether the cotton-seller is loyal or rebel, or whether he is paid in corn-meal or gunpowder.

(NH IX, 10)

July 4, 1863
On the morning of July 3, General Grant won a major victory when he forced the surrender of Confederate troops at Vicksburg, Mississippi, after a six-week siege. With the loss of the last stronghold on the Mississippi River, the Confederacy was split in two.

The President announces to his country that news from the Army of the Potomac, up to 10 P.M. of the 3d, is such as to cover that army with the highest honor, to promise a great success to the cause of the Union, and to claim the condolence of all for the many gallant fallen; and that for this he especially desires that on this day He whose will, not ours, should ever be done be everywhere remembered and reverenced with profoundest gratitude.

(NH IX, 17)

July 14, 1863
Following the Battle of Gettysburg (July 1–3), President Lincoln drafted a letter to General George G. Meade in which he criticized him for not pursuing the retreating Confederate army, a move that could have ended the war. The letter was never sent.

The case, summarily stated, is this: you fought and beat the enemy at Gettysburg and, of course, to say the least, his loss was as great as yours. He retreated, and you did not, as it seemed to me, pressingly pursue him; but a flood in the river detained him till, by slow degrees, you were again upon him. You had at least twenty thousand veteran troops directly with you, and as many more raw ones within supporting distance, all in addition to those who fought with you at Gettysburg, while it was not possible that he had received a single recruit, and yet you stood and let the flood run down, bridges be built, and the enemy move away at his leisure without attacking him. . . .

Again, my dear general, I do not believe you appreciate the magnitude of the misfortune involved in Lee's escape. He was within your easy grasp, and to have closed upon him would, in connection with our other late successes, have ended the war. As it is, the war will be prolonged indefinitely.

(NH IX, 28–29)

July 15, 1863
Proclamation on Thanksgiving Day, issued after the Union victories at Vicksburg and Gettysburg.

It has pleased Almighty God to hearken to the supplications and prayers of an afflicted people, and to vouchsafe to the army and navy of the United States victories on land and on sea so signal and so effective as to furnish reasonable grounds for augmented confidence that the union of these states will be maintained, their Constitution preserved, and their peace and prosperity permanently restored. But these victories have been accorded not without sacrifices of life, limb, health, and liberty, incurred by brave, loyal and patriotic citizens. Domestic affliction in every part of the country follows in the train of these fearful bereavements. It is meet and right to recognize and confess the presence of the Almighty Father and the power of His hand equally in these triumphs and in these sorrows.

Now, therefore, be it known that I do set apart Thursday, the 6th day of August next, to be observed as a day for national thanksgiving, praise, and prayer, and I invite the people of the United States to assemble on that occasion in their customary places of worship, and, in the forms approved by their own consciences, render the homage due to the Divine Majesty for the

wonderful things he has done in the nation's behalf, and invoke
the influence of his Holy Spirit to subdue the anger which has
produced and so long sustained a needless and cruel rebellion, to
change the hearts of the insurgents, to guide the counsels of the
government with wisdom adequate to so great a national emergency, and to visit with tender care and consolation throughout
the length and breadth of our land all those who, through the vi-
cissitudes of marches, voyages, battles, and sieges have been brought
to suffer in mind, body, or estate, and finally to lead the whole nation through the paths of repentance and submission to the Divine
Will back to the perfect enjoyment of union and fraternal peace.

(NH IX, 32–33)

July 21, 1863
Lincoln expressed his dissatisfaction with General Meade's ac-
tions following the victory at Gettysburg, but still supported him.

I was deeply mortified by the escape of Lee across the Potomac,
because the substantial destruction of his army would have ended
the war, and because I believed such destruction was perfectly
easy—believed that General Meade and his noble army had ex-
pended all the skill, and toil, and blood, up to the ripe harvest, and
then let the crop go to waste. . . .

General Meade has my confidence as a brave and skilful officer
and a true man.

(NH IX, 39)

July 30, 1863
Confederate mistreatment of captured U.S. Colored Troops led
Lincoln to draft an order of retaliation.

The law of nations, and the usages and customs of war, as carried
on by civilized powers, permit no distinction as to color in the
treatment of prisoners of war as public enemies. To sell or enslave
any captured person on account of his color, and for no offense
against the laws of war, is a relapse into barbarism and a crime

against the civilization of the age. The government of the United States will give the same protection to all its soldiers, and if the enemy shall sell or enslave anyone because of his color, the offense shall be punished by retaliation upon the enemy's prisoners in our possession.

It is therefore ordered that for every soldier of the United States killed in violation of the laws of war, a rebel soldier shall be executed; and for every one enslaved by the enemy or sold into slavery, a rebel soldier shall be placed at hard labor on the public works, and continued at such labor until the other shall be released and receive the treatment due to a prisoner of war.

(NH IX, 48–49)

August 7, 1863
Letter to Governor Joseph Gilmore of New Hampshire, stressing the importance of the draft.

I do not object to abide a decision of the United States Supreme Court, or of the judges thereof, on the constitutionality of the draft law. In fact, I should be willing to facilitate the obtaining of it, but I cannot consent to lose the time while it is being obtained. We are contending with an enemy, who, as I understand, drives every able-bodied man he can reach into his ranks, very much as a butcher drives bullocks into a slaughter-pen.

(NH IX, 60)

August 15, 1863
An opinion on the draft, which was never sent.

I do not say that all who would avoid serving in the war are unpatriotic; but I do think every patriot should willingly take his chance under a law made with great care, in order to secure entire fairness. . . . Much complaint is made of that provision of the conscription law which allows a drafted man to substitute three hundred dollars for himself; while, as I believe, none is made of that provision which allows him to substitute another man for himself. Nor is the three hundred dollar provision objected to for unconstitutionality; but for inequality, for favoring the rich against the poor.

(NH IX, 78–79)

September 19, 1863
In a letter to General Halleck, President Lincoln expressed his frustration that the numerically superior Union army could not deal a decisive defeat to the Confederates.

General Meade, as shown by the returns, has with him, and between him and Washington, of the same classes of well men, over 90,000. Neither can bring the whole of his men into a battle; but each can bring as large a percentage in as the other. For a battle, then, General Meade has three men to General Lee's two. Yet, it having been determined that choosing ground and standing on the defensive gives so great advantage that the three cannot safely attack the two, the three are left simply standing on the defensive also.

(NH IX, 128–29)

October 12, 1863
Telegram to General Rosecrans, who was pursuing General Robert E. Lee's Army of Virginia.

You and Burnside now have him by the throat; and he must break your hold or perish.

(NH IX, 167)

November 19, 1863
Lincoln's closing paragraph for the dedication of the Gettysburg National Cemetery. (See Appendix E for complete text.)

But, in a larger sense, we cannot dedicate—we cannot consecrate—we cannot hallow—this ground. The brave men, living and dead, who struggled here, have consecrated it far above our poor power to add or detract. The world will little note nor long remember what we say here, but it can never forget what they did here. It is for us, the living, rather, to be dedicated here to the unfinished work which they who fought here have thus far so nobly advanced. It is rather for us to be here dedicated to the great task remaining before us—that from these honored dead we take increased devotion to that cause for which they gave the last full measure of devotion; that we here highly resolve that these dead shall not have died in vain; that this nation, under God, shall have a new birth of freedom; and that government of the people, by the people, for the people, shall not perish from the earth.

(NH IX, 210)

November 20, 1863
From a letter to Edward Everett, the featured speaker at the dedication of the Gettysburg National Cemetery. Everett was considered one of the foremost public speakers of his day and gave an address that lasted over two hours. Lincoln's speech lasted only two minutes, but is considered one of the greatest American speeches of all time.

In our respective parts yesterday, you could not have been excused to make a short address, nor I a long one. I am pleased to know that, in your judgment, the little I did say was not entirely a failure.

(NH IX, 210–11)

December 8, 1863
Lincoln predicted that the Union navy, with its rapidly expanding fleet of steel armored ships, would play an important part in U.S. foreign policy after the war.

The naval force of the United States consists at this time of five hundred and eighty-eight vessels, completed and in the course of completion, and of these, seventy-five are iron-clad or armored steamers. The events of the war give an increased interest and importance to the navy which will probably extend beyond the war itself.

The armored vessels in our navy, completed and in service, or which are under contract and approaching completion, are believed to exceed in number those of any other power.

(NH IX, 236)

December 8, 1863
In his annual message to Congress, Lincoln defended his policy of emancipating the slaves.

The policy of emancipation, and of employing black soldiers, gave to the future a new aspect, about which hope, and fear, and doubt contended in uncertain conflict.... Eleven months having now passed, we are permitted to take another review. The rebel borders are pressed still further back, and, by the complete opening of the Mississippi, the country dominated by the rebellion is divided into distinct parts, with no practical communication between them. Tennessee and Arkansas have been substantially cleared of insurgent control, and influential citizens in each, owners of slaves and advocates of slavery at the beginning of the rebellion, now declare openly for emancipation in their respective states. Of those states not included in the Emancipation Proclamation, Maryland and Missouri, neither of which three years ago would tolerate any restraint upon the extension of slavery into new Territories, only dispute now as to the best mode of removing it within their own limits.

Of those who were slaves at the beginning of the rebellion, full one hundred thousand are now in the United States military service, about one half of which number actually bear arms in the ranks; thus giving the double advantage of taking so much labor from the insurgent cause, and supplying the places which otherwise must be filled with so many white men. So far as tested, it is difficult to say they are not as good soldiers as any.

(NH IX, 245–47)

January 7, 1864
President Lincoln stopped the execution of many Union troops charged with desertion and other offenses. He often reviewed individual cases involving the death sentence.

The death sentence of Henry Andrews is commuted to imprisonment at hard labor during the remainder of the war. . . . The case of Andrews is really a bad one, as appears by the record already before me. Yet before receiving this I had ordered his punishment commuted to imprisonment for during the war at hard labor, and had so telegraphed. I did this, not on any merit in this case, but because I am trying to evade the butchering business lately.

(NH IX, 279)

March 1, 1864
Letter to Secretary of War Stanton regarding an imprisoned soldier.

A poor widow, by the name of Baird, has a son in the army, that for some offense has been sentenced to serve a long time without pay, or at most with very little pay. I do not like this punishment of withholding pay—it falls so very hard upon poor families. After he had been serving this way for several months, at the tearful appeal of the poor mother, I made a direction that he be allowed to enlist for a new term, on the same conditions as others. She now comes, and says she cannot get it acted upon. Please do it.

(NH X, 27–28)

March 18, 1864
Remarks delivered at a Washington public fair organized by women to gather donations for Union troops.

I am not accustomed to the use of language of eulogy; I have never studied the art of paying compliments to women; but I must say, that if all that has been said by orators and poets since the creation of the world in praise of women were applied to the women of America, it would not do them justice for their conduct during this war. I will close by saying, God bless the women of America.

(NH X, 48–49)

April 18, 1864
At a fair in Baltimore, Maryland, Lincoln addressed news of a massacre of black troops at Fort Pillow.

A painful rumor—true, I fear—has reached us of the massacre by the rebel forces at Fort Pillow, in the west end of Tennessee, on the Mississippi River, of some three hundred soldiers and white officers, who had just been overpowered by their assailants. . . . At the beginning of the war, and for some time, the use of colored troops was not contemplated; and how the change of purpose was wrought I will not now take time to explain. Upon a clear conviction of duty I resolved to turn that element of strength to account; and I am responsible for it to the American people, to the Christian world, to history, and in my final account to God. Having determined to use the negro as a soldier, there is no way but to give him all the protection given to any other soldier.

(NH X, 79)

April 30, 1864
When General Hooker proved as ineffectual as his predecessors, President Lincoln removed him and appointed General Ulysses S. Grant. Lincoln trusted Grant implicitly and gave him tremendous leeway in all military matters.

The particulars of your plans I neither know nor seek to know. You are vigilant and self-reliant; and, pleased with this, I wish not to obtrude any constraints or restraints upon you. While I am very anxious that any great disaster or capture of our men in great numbers shall be avoided, I know these points are less likely to escape your attention than they would be mine. If there is anything wanting which is within my power to give, do not fail to let me know it.

(NH X, 90–91)

June 16, 1864
Shortly after accepting the Republican Party's nomination for a
second term, Lincoln discussed the ongoing war.

It is a pertinent question, often asked in the mind privately, and
from one to the other, when is the war to end? Surely I feel as
deep an interest in this question as any other can; but I do not
wish to name a day, a month, or year, when it is to end . . . This
war has taken three years; it was begun or accepted upon the line
of restoring the national authority over the whole national do-
main, and for the American people, as far as my knowledge enables me to speak, I say we are going through on this line if it
takes three years more.

(NH X, 129)

July 18, 1864
Due to devastating casualties in the Union army, Lincoln issued
a proclamation for another 500,000 troops.

I hereby proclaim, order, and direct, that immediately . . . a draft
for troops to serve for one year shall be had in every town, town-
ship, ward of a city, precinct or election district, or county not so
subdivided, to fill the quota which shall be assigned to it under
this call, or any part thereof which may be unfilled by volunteers
on the said fifth day of September, 1864.

(NH X, 165–66)

September 3, 1864
Following several significant military victories, including the
capture of Atlanta, Lincoln issued another Proclamation of
Thanksgiving.

The signal success that divine Providence has recently vouchsafed
to the operations of the United States fleet and army in the harbor
of Mobile, and the reduction of Fort Powell, Fort Gaines, and
Fort Morgan, and the glorious achievements of the army under
Major-General Sherman, in the state of Georgia, resulting in the

capture of the city of Atlanta, call for devout acknowledgment to the Supreme Being in whose hands are the destinies of nations.

(NH X, 211)

December 6, 1864
From Lincoln's last annual message to Congress.

I regard our immigrants as one of the principal replenishing streams which are appointed by Providence to repair the ravages of internal war, and its wastes of national strength and health.

(NH X, 291)

December 6, 1864
President Lincoln described recent military successes in his annual message.

The war continues. Since the last annual messages, all the important lines and positions then occupied by our forces have been maintained, and our arms have steadily advanced, thus liberating the regions left in rear; so that Missouri, Kentucky, Tennessee, and parts of other states again produced reasonably fair crops.

The most remarkable feature in the military operations of the year is General Sherman's attempted march of three hundred miles, directly through the insurgent region. It tends to show a great increase of our relative strength, that our general-in-chief should feel able to confront and hold in check every active force of the enemy, and yet to detach a well-appointed large army to move on such an expedition.

(NH X, 302–03)

December 6, 1864
Though casualty rates were extremely high, Lincoln knew that the North's numerical advantage would eventually lead to victory.

The election has exhibited another fact, not less valuable to be known—the fact that we do not approach exhaustion in the most important branch of national resources—that of living men. While it is melancholy to reflect that the war has filled so many graves, and carried mourning to so many hearts, it is some relief to know that compared with the surviving, the fallen have been so few. While corps, and divisions, and brigades, and regiments have formed, and fought, and dwindled, and gone out of existence, a great majority of the men who composed them are still living. . . . The important fact remains that we have more men now than we had when the war began; that we are not exhausted, nor in process of exhaustion; that we are gaining strength, and may, if need be, maintain the contest forever.

(NH X, 205–07)

December 26, 1864
Letter to General Sherman following his and Grant's successful campaign in Georgia.

Many, many thanks for your Christmas gift, the capture of Savannah.

When you were about leaving Atlanta for the Atlantic coast, I was anxious, if not fearful; but feeling that you were the better judge, and remembering that "nothing risked, nothing gained," I did not interfere. Now, the undertaking being a success, the honor is all yours; for I believe none of us went further than to acquiesce.

(NH X, 325)

March 17, 1865
Speaking to an Indiana regiment heading home from the war, Lincoln spoke about Confederate attempts to recruit black soldiers.

There are but few aspects of this great war on which I have not already expressed my views by speaking or writing. There is one—the recent effort of "our erring brethren," sometimes so called, to employ the slaves in their armies. The great question with them has been, "will the negro fight for them?" They ought to know better than we, and doubtless do know better than we. I may inci-

dentally remark, that having in my life heard many arguments—
or strings of words meant to pass for arguments—intended to
show that the negro ought to be a slave—if he shall now really
fight to keep himself a slave, it will be a far better argument why
he should remain a slave than I have ever before heard. He, perhaps, ought to be a slave if he desires it ardently enough to fight
for it. Or, if one out of four will, for his own freedom, fight to keep
the other three in slavery, he ought to be a slave for his selfish
meanness. I have always thought that all men should be free; but
if any should be slaves, it should be first those who desire it for
themselves, and secondly those who desire it for others. Whenever
I hear anyone arguing for slavery, I feel a strong impulse to see it
tried on him personally.

(NH XI, 55–56)

April 3, 1865
Secretary Stanton expressed concern over President Lincoln's de-
sire to visit Richmond, which had only recently been abandoned
by Confederate forces.

Thanks for your caution, but I have already been to Petersburg,
stayed with General Grant an hour and a half and returned here.
It is certain now that Richmond is in our hands, and I think I will
go there tomorrow. I will take care of myself.

(NH XI, 70)

April 7, 1865
General Lee's Army of Virginia retreated from Richmond in con-
fusion, with the Union army in hot pursuit.

Gen. Sheridan says "If the thing is pressed I think that Lee will
surrender." Let the *thing* be pressed.

(NH XI, 77)

April 11, 1865
From Lincoln's last public address, celebrating Lee's surrender on
April 9. Lincoln was shot five days later, and died on April 15,
1865.

We meet this evening not in sorrow, but in gladness of heart. The evacuation of Petersburg and Richmond, and the surrender of the principal insurgent army, give hope of a righteous and speedy peace, whose joyous expression cannot be restrained. In the midst of this, however, He from whom all blessings flow must not be forgotten. A call for a national thanksgiving is being prepared, and will be duly promulgated. Nor must those whose harder part gave us the cause of rejoicing be overlooked. Their honors must not be parceled out with the others. I myself was near the front, and had the high pleasure of transmitting much of the good news to you; but no part of the honor for plan or execution is mine. To General Grant, his skilful officers and brave men, all belongs.

(NH XI, 84)

Peace and Reconstruction

Long before the war ended, Lincoln began planning for the eventual peace. He knew that, with the North's tremendous economic and numerical advantage, it would only be a matter of time before the South would be forced to surrender. Despite the tremendous losses and hardships caused by the war, Lincoln was determined to fashion flexible terms that would not hurt or humiliate Southerners, but would treat them with dignity and respect. He stressed repeatedly that, even if a former Confederate refused to take an oath of loyalty, "it is enough if the man does no wrong hereafter." With Lincoln's assassination shortly after the end of the war, hopes for a generous reconciliation with the South suffered a devastating blow.

> *August 26, 1863*
> *Letter to J. C. Conkling, regarding the prospects for peace between North and South.*

Peace does not appear so distant as it did. I hope it will come soon, and come to stay; and so come as to be worth the keeping in all future time. It will then have been proved that among free men there can be no successful appeal from the ballot to the bullet, and that they who take such appeal are sure to lose their case and pay the cost. And then there will be some black men who can remember that with silent tongue, and clenched teeth, and steady eye, and well-poised bayonet, they have helped mankind on to this great consummation, while I fear there will be some white ones unable to forget that with malignant heart and deceitful speech they strove to hinder it.

(NH IX, 101–02)

September 11, 1863
Letter to Governor Andrew Johnson of Tennessee.

Let the reconstruction be the work of such men only as can be trusted for the Union. Exclude all others, and trust that your government so organized will be recognized here as being the one of republican form to be guaranteed to the state, and to be protected against invasion and domestic violence. It is something on the question of time to remember that it cannot be known who is next to occupy the position I now hold, nor what he will do.

(NH IX, 116–17)

October 1, 1863
From a letter to a Union general in charge of the newly reorganized state of Missouri.

Under your recent order, which I have approved, you will only arrest individuals and suppress assemblies or newspapers when they may be working palpable injury to the military in your charge, and in no other case will you interfere with the expression of opinion in any form or allow it to be interfered with violently by others. In this you have a discretion to exercise with great caution, calmness, and forbearance.

(NH IX, 148)

December 8, 1863
Long before the war ended, Lincoln issued a Proclamation for Amnesty and Reconstruction which contained two essential terms for peace with the South: the abolition of slavery and a loyalty oath. The proclamation excluded anyone serving in the Confederate government, officers in the Confederate army, former members of Congress who abandoned their posts to join the Confederate cause,

and anyone discovered to have mistreated African-American pri-
soners of war. The proclamation also encouraged the education of
former slaves.

I . . . declare, and make known to all persons who have, directly or
by implication, participated in the existing rebellion, except as
hereinafter excepted, that a full pardon is hereby granted to them
and each of them, with restoration of all rights of property, except
as to slaves, and in property cases where rights of third parties
shall have intervened, and upon the condition that every such person shall take and subscribe an oath, and thenceforward keep and
maintain said oath inviolate.

(NH IX, 219–20)

December 8, 1863
In his annual address to Congress, President Lincoln stated that
he was flexible regarding the proposed terms of reconstruction.

The objection to a premature presentation of a plan by the national executive consists in the danger of committals on points
which could be more safely left to further developments. Care has
been taken to so shape the document as to avoid embarrassments
from this source. Saying that, on certain terms, certain classes will
be pardoned, with rights restored, it is not said that other classes,
or other terms will never be included. Saying that reconstruction
will be accepted if presented in a specified way, it is not said it will
never be accepted in any other way. . . . In the midst of other cares,
however important, we must not lose sight of the fact that the war
power is still our main reliance. To that power alone can we look,
yet for a time, to give confidence to the people in the contested regions that the insurgent power will not again overrun them. Until
that confidence shall be established, little can be done anywhere
for what is called reconstruction.

(NH IX, 251–52)

December 14, 1863
From the amnesty declaration for Emily Todd Helm, a half-sister of Mary Todd Lincoln, given after she took the loyalty oath.

Mrs. Emily T. Helm, not being excepted from the benefits of the proclamation by the President of the United States issued on the eighth day of December, 1863, and having on this day taken and subscribed the oath according to said proclamation, she is full relieved of all penalties and forfeitures, and remitted to all her rights—all according to said proclamation, and not otherwise; and, in regard to said restored rights of person and property, she is to be protected and afforded facilities as a loyal person.

(NH IX, 255)

December 15, 1863
From a letter regarding the plans for a new state government in Louisiana.

The strongest wish I have, not already publicly expressed, is that in Louisiana and elsewhere all sincere Union men would stoutly eschew cliquism, and, each yielding something in minor matters, all work together. Nothing is likely to be so baleful in the great work before us as stepping aside from the main object to consider who will get the offices if a small matter shall go thus, and who else will get them if it shall go otherwise. It is a time now for real patriots to rise above all this.

(NH IX, 257)

January 16, 1864
Letter to the editors of a publication which carried a mistaken explanation of Lincoln's stand on reconstruction.

The sentence of twelve lines, commencing at the top of page 252, I could wish to be not exactly as it is. I have never had a theory that secession could absolve states or people from their obligations. Precisely the contrary is asserted in the inaugural address; and it was because of my belief in the continuation of these *oblig-*

ations that I was puzzled, for a time, as to denying the legal *rights* of those citizens who remained individually innocent of treason or rebellion.

(NH IX, 285)

February 5, 1864
Note on the loyalty oath to Secretary of War Stanton.

On principle I dislike an oath which requires a man to swear he has not done wrong. It rejects the Christian principle of forgiveness on terms of repentance. I think it is enough if the man does no wrong hereafter.

(NH IX, 303)

April 4, 1864
President Lincoln became very concerned when Union General William S. Rosecrans, the federally appointed head of the new military administration in Missouri, began demanding a loyalty oath from all religious groups in the state.

I somewhat dread the effect of your Special Order No. 61, dated March 7, 1864. I have found that men who have not even been suspected of disloyalty are very averse to taking an oath of any sort as a condition to exercising an ordinary right of citizenship. The point will probably be made that while men may, without an oath, assemble in a noisy political meeting, they must take the oath to assemble in a religious meeting.

(NH X, 63–64)

July 8, 1864
Proclamation concerning reconstruction.

I, Abraham Lincoln, President of the United States, do proclaim . . . that while I am . . . unprepared . . . to be inflexibly committed to any single plan of restoration; and, while I am also unprepared to declare that the free-state constitutions and governments already adopted and installed in Arkansas and Louisiana shall be set aside and held for naught, thereby repelling and discouraging the loyal citizens who have set up the same as to further effort, or to declare a constitutional competency in Congress to abolish slavery in states, but am at the same time sincerely hoping and expecting that a constitutional amendment abolishing slavery throughout the nation may be adopted, nevertheless I am fully satisfied with the system for restoration contained in the bill as one very proper plan for the loyal people of any state choosing to adopt it, and that I am, and at all times shall be, prepared to give the executive aid and assistance to any such people, so soon as the military resistance to the United States shall have been suppressed in any such state, and the people thereof shall have sufficiently returned to their obedience to the Constitution and the laws of the United States, in which cases military governors will be appointed, with directions to proceed according to the bill.

(NH X, 152–53)

July 18, 1864
Lincoln's terms of peace, which were intended for Confederate negotiators.

Any proposition which embraces the restoration of peace, the integrity of the whole Union, and the abandonment of slavery, and which comes by and with an authority that can control the armies now at war against the United States, will be received and considered by the executive government of the United States, and will be met by liberal terms on other substantial and collateral points, and the bearer or bearers thereof shall have safe conduct both ways.

(NH X, 161)

December 6, 1864
An account of new state governments established in formerly Confederate states, from the annual message to Congress.

Important movements have also occurred during the year to the effect of molding society for durability in the Union. Although short of complete success, it is much in the right direction that 12,000 citizens in each of the states of Arkansas and Louisiana have organized loyal state governments, with free constitutions, and are earnestly struggling to maintain and administer them. The movements in the same direction, more extensive though less definite, in Missouri, Kentucky, and Tennessee, should not be overlooked. But Maryland presents the example of complete success. Maryland is secure to liberty and Union for all the future. The genius of rebellion will no more claim Maryland. Like another foul spirit, being driven out, it may seek to tear her, but it will woo her no more.

(NH X, 303)

December 6, 1864
Although he never mentioned Confederate President Jefferson Davis by name, Lincoln alluded to him in his annual address to Congress.

On careful consideration of all the evidence accessible, it seems to me that no attempt at negotiating with the insurgent leader could result in any good. He would accept nothing short of severance of the Union—precisely what we will not and cannot give. His declarations to this effect are explicit and oft repeated. He does not attempt to deceive us. He affords us no excuse to deceive ourselves.

(HN X, 307–08)

March 4, 1865
The closing words of Lincoln's second inaugural address. (See Appendix G for complete text.)

Fondly we hope—fervently do we pray—that this mighty scourge of war may speedily pass away. Yet, if God wills that it continue until all the wealth piled by the bondsman's two hundred and fifty years of unrequited toil shall be sunk, and until every drop of blood drawn with the lash shall be paid by another drawn with the sword, as was said three thousand years ago, so still it must be said, "The judgments of the Lord are true and righteous altogether."

With malice toward none; with charity for all; with firmness in the right, as God gives us to see the right, let us strive on to finish the work we are in; to bind up the nation's wounds; to care for him who shall have borne the battle, and for his widow, and his orphan—to do all which may achieve and cherish a just and lasting peace among ourselves, and with all nations.

(NH XI, 46–47)

April 11, 1865
On April 9, 1865, General Lee surrendered at Appomattox, thus ending the Civil War. In his last public address, Lincoln discussed the difficult road ahead.

By the recent successes the reinauguration of the national authority—reconstruction—which has had a large share of thought from the first, is pressed much more closely upon our attention. It is fraught with great difficulty. Unlike a case of war between independent nations, there is no authorized organ for us to treat with—no man has authority to give up the rebellion for any other man. We simply must begin with and mold from disorganized and discordant elements. Nor is it a small additional embarrassment that we, the loyal people, differ among ourselves as to the mode, manner, and measure of reconstruction. . . . We all agree that the seceded states, so called, are out of their proper practical relation with the Union, and that the sole object of the government, civil and military, in regard to those states, is to again get them into that proper practical relation. . . . Let us all join in doing the acts necessary to restoring the proper practical relations between these states and the Union, and each forever after innocently indulge his own opinion whether in doing the acts he brought the states from without into the Union, or only gave them proper assistance, they never having been out of it.

(NH XI, 85–88)

April 14, 1865
In his last letter, written the day he was shot, President Lincoln thanked one of his supporters, General Van Alen.

I thank you for the assurance you give me that I shall be supported by conservative men like yourself, in the efforts I may make to restore the Union, so as to make it, to use your language, a Union of hearts and hands as well as of states.

(NH XI, 94)

PART III

Slavery and Emancipation

Abraham Lincoln was, by the standards of his day, a moderate on the volatile question of slavery. Although he described the institution of slavery as a "monstrous injustice," he knew that it was political suicide to take up the radical abolitionist cause, favoring instead those policies that he thought would lead to slavery's peaceful extinction. He admired the spirit of compromise embodied by his political hero, Henry Clay, and, like Clay, advocated gradual emancipation. Lincoln supported colonization efforts, but recognized that the economics of ridding the entire country of enslaved and free blacks was completely unfeasible. As the Civil War wore on, lobbying efforts by Frederick Douglass and others in the abolition movement led Lincoln to issue the Emancipation Proclamation, which freed all slaves in rebellious territories and cleared the way for the establishment of the United States Colored Troops (U.S.C.T.). Lincoln lobbied Congress for passage of the Thirteenth Amendment, but he died seven months before its ratification.

> *September 27, 1841*
> *In a letter to Mary Speed, Lincoln recounted the effect of seeing slaves being transported in Kentucky.*

By the way, a fine example was presented on board the boat for contemplating the effect of condition upon human happiness. A gentleman had purchased twelve negroes in different parts of Kentucky, and was taking them to a farm in the South. They were chained six and six together. A small iron clevis was around the left wrist of each, and this was fastened to the main chain by a shorter one, at a convenient distance from the others, so that the negroes were strung together precisely like so many fish upon a trotline. In this condition they were being separated forever from the scenes of their childhood, their friends, their fathers and mothers, and their wives and children, and going into perpetual slavery, where the lash of the master is proverbially more ruthless and unrelenting than any other where; and yet amid all these distressing circumstances, as we would think them, they were the most cheerful and apparently happy creatures on board. One whose offense for which he had been sold was an over-fondness for his wife, played the fiddle almost continually, and the others danced, sang, cracked jokes, and played various games with cards from day to day. How true it is that "God tempers the wind to the shorn lamb," or in other words, that he renders the worst of human conditions tolerable, while he permits the best to be nothing better than tolerable.

(NH I, 178–79)

October 3, 1845
Lincoln questioned members of the Liberty Party, which caused a split in antislavery forces and thus contributed to the election of President James K. Polk, a slaveholder.

If by your votes you could have prevented the extension, etc. of slavery, would it not have been good, and not evil, so to have used your votes, even though it involved the casting of them for a slaveholder? By the fruit the tree is to be known. An evil tree cannot bring forth good fruit. If the fruit of electing Mr. Clay would have been to prevent the extension of slavery, could the act of electing have been evil?

(NH I, 276)

October 3, 1845
A summary of Lincoln's views on slavery, during his career in the
Illinois legislature.

I hold it to be a paramount duty of us in the free states, due to the
Union of the States, and perhaps to liberty itself (paradox though
it may seem), to let the slavery of the other states alone; while, on
the other hand, I hold it to be equally clear that we should never
knowingly lend ourselves, directly or indirectly, to prevent that
slavery from dying a natural death—to find new places for it to
live in, when it can no longer exist in the old.

(NH I, 277)

July 16, 1852
From Lincoln's eulogy for Henry Clay, the American statesman
and orator who authored the Missouri Compromise.

Those who would shiver into fragments the Union of these states,
tear to tatters its now venerated Constitution, and even burn the
last copy of the Bible, rather than slavery should continue a single
hour, together with all their more halting sympathizers, have received, and are receiving, their just execration; and the name and
opinions and influence of Mr. Clay are fully and, as I trust, effectually and enduringly arrayed against them. But I would also, if I
could, array his name, opinions, and influence against the opposite
extreme—against a few but an increasing number of men who, for
the sake of perpetuating slavery, are beginning to assail and to
ridicule the white man's charter of freedom, the declaration that
"all men are created free and equal."

(NH II, 172–73)

July 16, 1852
From the eulogy for Henry Clay.

Pharaoh's country was plagued, and his hosts were lost in the Red
Sea, for striving to retain a captive people who had already served
them more than four hundred years. May like disasters never be-

fall us! If, as the friends of colonization hope, the present and coming generations of our countrymen shall by any means succeed in freeing our land from the dangerous presence of slavery, and at the same time in restoring a captive people to their long-lost fatherland with bright prospects for the future, and this too so gradually that neither races nor individuals shall have suffered by the change, it will indeed be a glorious consummation.

(NH II, 176–77)

July 1, 1854
Part of a fragment on slavery.

The ant who has toiled and dragged a crumb to his nest will furiously defend the fruit of his labor against whatever robber assails him. So plain that the most dumb and stupid slave that ever toiled for a master does constantly know that he is wronged. So plain that no one, high or low, ever does mistake it, except in a plainly selfish way; for although volume upon volume is written to prove slavery a very good thing, we never hear of the man who wishes to take the good of it by being a slave himself.

(NH II, 183–84)

October 16, 1854
In one of the speeches that defined his political career, Lincoln argued against the recent repeal of the Missouri Compromise.

The declared indifference, but, as I must think, covert real zeal, for the spread of slavery, I cannot but hate. I hate it because of the monstrous injustice of slavery itself. I hate it because it deprives our republican example of its just influence in the world; enables the enemies of free institutions with plausibility to taunt us as hypocrites; causes the real friends of freedom to doubt our sincerity; and especially because it forces so many good men among ourselves into an open war with the very fundamental principles of civil liberty, criticizing the Declaration of Independence, and insisting that there is no right principle of action but self interest.

(NH II, 205)

October 16, 1854
Lincoln explored solutions to the problem of slavery at Peoria,
Illinois.

My first impulse would be to free all the slaves, and send them to Liberia, to their own native land. But a moment's reflection would convince me that whatever of high hope (as I think there is) there may be in this in the long run, its sudden execution is impossible. If they were all landed there in a day, they would all perish in the next ten days; and there are not surplus shipping and surplus money enough to carry them there in many times ten days. . . . What next? Free them, and make them politically and socially our equals. My own feelings will not admit of this, and if mine would, we well know that those of the great mass of whites will not. Whether this feeling accords with justice and sound judgment is not the sole question, if indeed it is any part of it. A universal feeling, whether well or ill founded, cannot be safely disregarded. We cannot then make them equals. It does seem to me that systems of gradual emancipation might be adopted, but for their tardiness in this I will not undertake to judge our brethren of the South.

(NH II, 206–07)

October 16, 1854
Lincoln countered the argument advanced by Stephen A.
Douglas, that slavery was protected by the principle of self-
government.

When the white man governs himself, that is self-government; but when he governs himself and also governs another man, that is more than self-government—that is despotism. If the negro is a man, why then my ancient faith teaches me that "all men are created equal," and that there can be no moral right in connection with one man's making a slave of another.

(NH II, 227–28)

October 16, 1854
From the speech in Peoria, Illinois.

I insist that whether I shall be a whole man, or only the half of one, in comparison with others, is a question in which I am somewhat concerned, and one which no other man can have a sacred right of deciding for me.

(NH II, 235)

October 16, 1854
A summary of Lincoln's view on the repeal of the Missouri Compromise.

Much as I hate slavery, I would consent to the extension of it rather than see the Union dissolved, just as I would consent to any great evil to avoid a greater one. But when I go to Union-saving, I must believe, at least, that the means I employ have some adaptation to the end. To my mind, Nebraska has no such adaptation. . . . Repeal the Missouri Compromise, repeal all compromises, repeal the Declaration of Independence, repeal all past history, you still cannot repeal human nature. It still will be the abundance of man's heart that slavery extension is wrong, and out of the abundance of his heart his mouth will continue to speak.

(NH II, 236–38)

October 16, 1854
Lincoln's opinion on slavery, from the speech in Peoria, Illinois.

Near eighty years ago we began by declaring that all men are created equal; but now from that beginning we have run down to the other declaration, that for some men to enslave others is a "sacred right of self-government." These principles cannot stand together. They are as opposite as God and Mammon; and whoever holds to the one must despise the other.

(NH II, 246–47)

August 15, 1855
Letter to George Robertson, a former member of Congress who
spoke of "the peaceful extinction of slavery" more than three
decades earlier.

Since then we have had thirty-six years of experience; and this experience has demonstrated, I think, that there is no peaceful extinction of slavery in prospect for us. The signal failure of Henry
Clay, and other good and great men, in 1849, to effect any thing
in favor of gradual emancipation in Kentucky, together with a
thousand other signs, extinguishes that hope utterly. When we
were the political slaves of King George, and wanted to be free, we
called the maxim that "all men are created equal" a self evident
truth; but now when we have grown fat, and have lost all dread of
being slaves ourselves, we have become so greedy to be masters
that we call the same maxim "a self evident lie." The fourth of July
has not quite dwindled away; it is still a great day—for burning
fire-crackers!!!

(CW II, 318)

August 15, 1855
Letter to George Robertson, in which Lincoln used language sim-
ilar to that employed in his later "House Divided" speech.

Our political problem now is, "Can we, as a nation, continue together permanently—forever—half slave and half free?" The
problem is too mighty for me—may God, in his mercy, superin-
tend the solution.

(CW II, 318)

August 24, 1855
Letter to Joshua Speed, in which Lincoln recounted the experience
that crystallized his feelings toward slavery.

You may remember, as I well do, that from Louisville to the
mouth of the Ohio there were on board ten or a dozen slaves

shackled together with irons. That sight was a continued torment to me, and I see something like it every time I touch the Ohio or any other slave border.

(NH II, 282)

August 27, 1856
From a speech at a Republican gathering in Kalamazoo, Michigan.

The question of slavery, at the present day, should be not only the greatest question, but very nearly the sole question.

(CW II, 361)

June 26, 1857
From a speech on the Supreme Court's Dred Scott decision.

Chief Justice Taney, in delivering the opinion of the majority of the Court, insists at great length that negroes were no part of the people who made, or for whom was made, the Declaration of Independence, or the Constitution of the United States.

On the contrary, Judge Curtis, in his dissenting opinion, shows that in five of the then thirteen states, to wit, New Hampshire, Massachusetts, New York, New Jersey and North Carolina, free negroes were voters, and, in proportion to their numbers, had the same part in making the Constitution that the white people had.

(CW II, 403)

June 26, 1857
An account of slavery and the condition of enslaved African-Americans, from Lincoln's speech on the Dred Scott decision.

In some trifling particulars, the condition of that race has been ameliorated; but, as a whole, in this country, the change between then and now is decidedly the other way; and their ultimate destiny has never appeared so hopeless as in the last three or four years. In two of the five states—New Jersey and North Carolina—that then gave the free negro the right of voting, it has since been taken away; and in a third—New York—it has been greatly abridged; while it has not been extended, so far as I know, to a single additional state, though the number of the states has more than doubled. In those days, as I understand, masters could, at their own pleasure, emancipate their slaves; but since then, such legal restraints have been made upon emancipation, as to amount almost to prohibition. In those days, legislatures held the unquestioned power to abolish slavery in their respective states; but now it is becoming quite fashionable for state constitutions to withhold that power from the legislatures. In those days, by common consent, the spread of the black man's bondage to the new countries was prohibited; but now, Congress decides that it will not continue the prohibition, and the Supreme Court decides that it could not if it would. In those days, our Declaration of Independence was held sacred by all, and thought to include all; but now, to aid in making the bondage of the negro universal and eternal, it is assailed, and sneered at, and construed, and hawked at, and torn, till, if its framers could rise from their graves, they could not at all recognize it. All the powers of earth seem rapidly combining against him. Mammon is after him; ambition follows, and philosophy follows, and the theology of the day is fast joining the cry. They have him in his prison house; they have searched his person, and left no prying instrument with him. One after another they have closed the heavy iron doors upon him, and now they have him, as it were, bolted in with a lock of a hundred keys, which can never be unlocked without the concurrence of every key; the keys in the hands of a hundred different men, and they scattered to a hundred different and distant places; and they stand musing as to what invention in all the dominions of mind and matter, can be produced to make the impossibility of his escape more complete than it is.

(CW II, 403–04)

June 26, 1857
Lincoln argued against Stephen A. Douglas and others who
claimed that African-Americans were excluded from the state-
ment in the Declaration of Independence that "all men are created
equal."

He finds the Republicans insisting that the Declaration of
Independence includes all men, black as well as white; and forth-
with he boldly denies that it includes negroes at all, and proceeds
to argue gravely that all who contend it does, do so only because
they want to vote, and eat, and sleep, and marry with negroes! . . .
Now I protest against the counterfeit logic which concludes that,
because I do not want a black woman for a slave I must necessarily want her for a wife. I need not have her for either, I can just
leave her alone. In some respects she certainly is not my equal; but
in her natural right to eat the bread she earns with her own hands
without asking leave of anyone else, she is my equal, and the equal
of all others.

(CW II, 405)

June 26, 1857
The intent of the Declaration of Independence, as interpreted by
Lincoln.

Chief Justice Taney, in his opinion in the Dred Scott case, admits
that the language of the Declaration is broad enough to include
the whole human family, but he and Judge Douglas argue that the
authors of that instrument did not intend to include negroes, by
the fact that they did not at once actually place them on an equality with whites. Now this grave argument comes to just nothing at
all, by the other fact that they did not at once, or ever afterward,
actually place all white people on an equality with one another.
And this is the staple argument of both the Chief Justice and the
Senator for doing this obvious violence to the plain, unmistakable
language of the Declaration. I think the authors of that notable

instrument intended to include all men, but they did not intend to declare all men equal in all respects. They did not mean to say all were equal in color, size, intellect, moral developments, or social capacity. They defined with tolerable distinctness, in what respects they did consider all men created equal—equal with "certain inalienable rights, among which are life, liberty, and the pursuit of happiness." This they said, and this they meant. They did not mean to assert the obvious untruth, that all were then actually enjoying that equality, nor yet, that they were about to confer it immediately upon them. In fact, they had no power to confer such a boon. They meant simply to declare the right, so that enforcement of it might follow as fast as circumstances should permit. They meant to set up a standard maxim for free society, which should be familiar to all, and revered by all; constantly looked to, constantly labored for, and even though never attained, constantly approximated, and thereby constantly spreading and deepening its influence, and augmenting the happiness and value of life to all people of all colors everywhere.

(CW II, 405–06)

June 26, 1857
Fears of racial mixing were very prevalent in the nineteenth century. Lincoln's stance was considered moderate by contemporary standards.

But Judge Douglas is especially horrified at the thought of the mixing of blood by the white and black races: agreed for once—a thousand times agreed. There are white men enough to marry all the white women, and black men enough to marry all the black women; and so let them be married. On this point we fully agree with the judge; and when he shall show that his policy is better adapted to prevent amalgamation than ours we shall drop ours, and adopt his.

(CW II, 408)

June 26, 1857
A summary of the difference between the two major political parties.

The Republicans inculcate, with whatever of ability they can, that the negro is a man; that his bondage is cruelly wrong, and that the field of his oppression ought not to be enlarged. The Democrats deny his manhood; deny, or dwarf to insignificance, the wrong of his bondage; so far as possible, crush all sympathy for him; and cultivate and excite hatred and disgust against him; compliment themselves as Union-savers for doing so; and call the indefinite outspreading of his bondage "a sacred right of self-government."

(CW II, 409)

July 1858
Part of a fragment on slavery.

I have not allowed myself to forget that the abolition of the slave trade by Great Britain was agitated a hundred years before it was a final success; that the measure had its open fire-eating opponents; its stealthy "don't care" opponents; its dollar and cent opponents; its inferior race opponents; its negro equality opponents; and its religion and good order opponents; that all these opponents got offices, and their adversaries got none. But I have also remembered that though they blazed, like tallow candles for a century, at last they flickered in the socket, died out, stank in the dark for a brief season, and were remembered no more, even by the smell. . . . Remembering these things, I cannot but regard it as possible that the higher object of this contest may not be completely attained within the term of my natural life. But I can not doubt either that it will come in due time. Even in this view, I am proud, in my passing speck of time, to contribute a humble mite to that glorious consummation, which my own poor eyes may not last to see.

(CW II, 482)

July 10, 1858
During a speech in Chicago, Lincoln argued against the Lecompton Constitution, which was designed to protect slavery in the newly organized state of Kansas.

Those arguments that are made, that the inferior race are to be treated with as much allowance as they are capable of enjoying; that as much is to be done for them as their condition will allow— what are these arguments? They are the arguments that kings have made for enslaving the people in all ages of the world. You will find that all the arguments in favor of kingcraft were of this class; they always bestrode the necks of the people—not that they wanted to do it, but because the people were better off for being ridden. That is their argument, and this argument of the judge is the same old serpent that says, you work and I eat, you toil and I will enjoy the fruits of it. Turn in whatever way you will—whether it come from the mouth of a king, an excuse for enslaving the people of his country, or from the mouth of men of one race as a reason for enslaving the men of another race, it is all the same old serpent, and I hold if that course of argumentation that is made for the purpose of convincing the public mind that we should not care about this should be granted, it does not stop with the negro.

(NH III, 49)

July 10, 1858
Near the close of his speech in Chicago, Lincoln reiterated his desire that African-Americans be granted equality.

My friends, I have detained you about as long as I desired to do, and I have only to say, let us discard all this quibbling about this man and the other man, this race and that race and the other race being inferior, and therefore they must be placed in an inferior position. Let us discard all these things, and unite as one people throughout this land, until we shall once more stand up declaring that all men are created equal.

(NH III, 51)

August 10, 1858
During his first debate with Stephen Douglas, Lincoln seemed to retreat from his pro-equality position.

I have no purpose to introduce political and social equality between the white and the black races. There is a physical difference between the two, which, in my judgment, will probably forever forbid their living together upon the footing of perfect equality; and inasmuch as it becomes a necessity that there must be a difference, I, as well as Judge Douglas, am in favor of the race to which I belong having the superior position.

(NH III, 239)

August 10, 1858
Lincoln's closing statement during the first debate with Stephen Douglas.

Judge Douglas is going back to the era of our Revolution, and to the extent of his ability muzzling the cannon which thunders its annual joyous return. When he invites any people, willing to have slavery, to establish it, he is blowing out the moral lights around us. When he says he "cares not whether slavery is voted down or voted up"—that it is the sacred right of self government—he is, in my judgment, penetrating the human soul and eradicating the light of reason and the lover of liberty in this American people.

(NH III, 256)

October 15, 1858
Lincoln's reply to Douglas during their last debate, in which he referred to slavery references contained in the Constitution.

In all three of these places, being the only allusion to slavery in the instrument, covert language is used. Language is used not suggesting that slavery existed or that the black race were among us. And I understand the contemporaneous history of those times to be that covert language was used with a purpose, and that purpose was that in our Constitution, which it was hoped, and is still hoped, will endure forever—when it should be read by intelligent and patriotic men, after the institution of slavery had passed from among us—there should be nothing on the face of the great charter of liberty suggesting that such a thing as negro slavery had ever existed among us.

(NH V, 49)

October 15, 1858
The Republican Party's position on slavery, from the final debate with Douglas.

The real issue in this controversy—the one pressing upon every mind—is the sentiment on the part of one class that looks upon the institution of slavery as a wrong, and of another class that does not look upon it as a wrong. The sentiment that contemplates the institution of slavery in this country as a wrong is the sentiment of the Republican party. It is the sentiment around which all their actions, all their arguments, circle; from which all their propositions radiate.

(NH V, 59–60)

October 15, 1858
In the last Lincoln-Douglas debate, Lincoln drew parallels between British oppression of the colonies and Southern arguments for slavery.

No matter in what shape it comes, whether from the mouth of a king who seeks to bestride the people of his own nation and live by the fruit of their labor, or from one race of men as an apology for enslaving another race, it is the same tyrannical principle.

(NH V, 65)

March 1, 1859
From a speech in Chicago.

The Republican principle, the profound central truth that slavery is wrong and ought to be dealt with as a wrong, though we are always to remember the fact of its actual existence amongst us and faithfully observe all the constitutional guarantees—the unalterable principle never for a moment to be lost sight of that it is a wrong and ought to be dealt with as such, cannot advance at all upon Judge Douglas' ground—that there is a portion of the country in which slavery must always exist; that he does not care whether it is voted up or voted down, as it is simply a question of dollars and cents. Whenever, in any compromise or arrangement or combination that may promise some temporary advantage, we are led upon that ground, then and there the great living principle upon which we have organized as a party is surrendered. The proposition now in our minds that this thing is wrong being once driven out and surrendered, then the institution of slavery necessarily becomes national.

(CW III, 368)

April 16, 1859
A comment on Jefferson's wording of the Declaration of Independence.

This is a world of compensation; and he who would be no slave must consent to have no slave. Those who deny freedom to others deserve it not for themselves, and, under a just God, cannot long retain it. All honor to Jefferson—to the man, who, in the concrete pressure of a struggle for national independence by a single people, had the coolness, forecast, and capacity to introduce into a merely revolutionary document an abstract truth, applicable to all men and all times, and so to embalm it there that today and in all coming days it shall be a rebuke and a stumbling block to the very harbingers of reappearing tyranny and oppression.

(NH V, 126–27)

September 17, 1859
A fragment on free labor, in which Lincoln countered pro-slavery arguments.

Equality in society alike beats inequality, whether the latter be of the British aristocratic sort or of the domestic slavery sort.

We know Southern men declare that their slaves are better off than hired laborers amongst us. How little they know, whereof they speak! There is no permanent class of hired laborers amongst us. Twenty-five years ago I was a hired laborer. The hired laborer of yesterday labors on his own account today, and will hire others to labor for him tomorrow. Advancement—improvement in condition—is the order of things in a society of equals. As labor is the common burthen of our race, so the effort of some to shift their share of the burden onto the shoulders of others, is the great, durable, curse of the race. Originally a curse for transgression upon the whole race, when, as by slavery, it is concentrated on a part only, it becomes the double-refined curse of God upon his creatures.

(CW III, 462)

February 27, 1860
From an address at the Cooper Institute, New York, in which Lincoln placed John Brown's slave insurrection in historical context.

That affair, in its philosophy, corresponds with the many attempts, related in history, at the assassination of kings and emperors. An enthusiast broods over the oppression of a people till he fancies himself commissioned by Heaven to liberate them. He ventures the attempt, which ends in little else than his own execution. Orsini's attempt on Louis Napoleon, and John Brown's attempt at Harper's Ferry, were, in their philosophy, precisely the same.

(NH V, 318–19)

March 5, 1860
From a speech in Hartford, Connecticut.

I think that if anything can be proved by natural theology, it is that slavery is morally wrong. God gave man a mouth to receive bread, hands to feed it, and his hand has a right to carry bread to his mouth without controversy.

(CW IV, 3)

March 6, 1860
From another speech in Hartford, Connecticut.

I want every man to have a chance—and I believe a black man is entitled to it—in which he can better his condition—when he may look forward and hope to be a hired laborer this year and the next, work for himself afterward, and finally to hire men to work for him. That is the true system.

(NH V, 361)

October 23, 1860
After Lincoln was nominated for the presidency, he was asked to reiterate his stand on slavery.

I have already done this many, many times; and it is in print, and open to all who will read. Those who will not read or heed what I have already publicly said would not read or heed a repetition of it. "If they hear not Moses and the prophets, neither will they be persuaded though one rose from the dead."

(NH VI, 63–64)

February 1, 1861
Prior to his inauguration, President-elect Lincoln wrote to his future Secretary of State, William H. Seward.

I say now . . . that on the territorial question—that is, the question of extending slavery under the national auspices—I am inflexible. I am for no compromise which assists or permits the extension of the institution on soil owned by the nation. And any trick by which the nation is to acquire territory, and then allow some local authority to spread slavery over it, is as obnoxious as any other.

I take it that to effect some such result as this, and to put us again on the high-road to a slave empire is the object of all these proposed compromises. I am against it.

As to fugitive slaves, District of Columbia, slave trade among the slave states, and whatever springs of necessity from the fact that the institution is amongst us, I care but little, so that what is done be comely, and not altogether outrageous. Nor do I care much about New Mexico, if further extension were hedged against.

(CW IV, 183)

March 4, 1861
From Lincoln's first inaugural address. (See Appendix C for complete text.)

One section of our country believes slavery is right, and ought to be extended, while the other believes it is wrong, and ought not to be extended. This is the only substantial dispute. The fugitive slave clause of the Constitution, and the law for the suppression of the foreign slave trade, are each as well enforced, perhaps, as any law can ever be in a community where the moral sense of the people imperfectly supports the law itself. The great body of the people abide by the dry legal obligation in both cases, and a few break over in each. This, I think, cannot be perfectly cured; and it would be worse in both cases after the separation of the sections than before. The foreign slave trade, now imperfectly suppressed, would be ultimately revived, without restriction, in one section, while fugitive slaves, now only partially surrendered, would not be surrendered at all by the other.

(NH VI, 180–81)

September 2, 1861
During the first few months of the Civil War, Lincoln was faced with the thorny issue of how to treat Southern slaves who crossed over Union lines. General John Fremont attempted to declare them free in a proclamation that he issued without proper authority.

I think there is great danger that the closing paragraph, in relation to the confiscation of property and the liberating slaves of traitorous owners, will alarm our southern Union friends and turn them against us; perhaps ruin our rather fair prospect for Kentucky.

(NH VI, 351)

December 3, 1861
A report on efforts to stop slave trade, from the annual message to
Congress.

The execution of the laws for the suppression of the African slave trade has been confided to the Department of the Interior. It is a subject of gratulation that the efforts which have been made for the suppression of this inhuman traffic have been recently attended with unusual success. Five vessels being fitted out for the slave trade have been seized and condemned. Two mates of vessels engaged in the trade, and one person in equipping a vessel as a slaver, have been convicted and subjected to the penalty of fine and imprisonment, and one captain, taken with a cargo of Africans on board his vessel, has been convicted of the highest grade of offense under our laws, the punishment of which is death.

(NH VII, 47–48)

December 3, 1861
Lincoln addressed the complex problem of Southern slaves liberated by the advancing Union army in his annual message to Congress.

Under and by virtue of the act of Congress entitled "An act to confiscate property used for insurrectionary purposes," approved August 6, 1861, the legal claims of certain persons to the labor and service of certain other persons have become forfeited; and numbers of the latter, thus liberated, are already dependent on the United States, and must be provided for in some way. Besides this, it is not impossible that some of the states will pass similar enactments for their own benefit respectively, and by operation of which persons of the same class will be thrown upon them for disposal. In such case I recommend that Congress provide for accepting such persons from such states, according to some mode of valuation, in lieu, *pro tanto*, of direct taxes, or upon some other plan to be agreed on with such states respectively; that such persons, on such acceptance by the general government, be at once deemed free; and that, in any event, steps be taken for colonizing both classes (or the one first mentioned, if the other shall not be brought into existence) at some place or places in a climate congenial to them. It might be well to consider, too, whether the free colored people already in the United States could not, so far as individuals may desire, be included in such colonization.

(NH VII, 49–50)

May 19, 1862
One of Lincoln's generals acted without proper authority when he declared the slaves in Georgia, Florida, and South Carolina free. Fearing a backlash from the Border States, Lincoln revoked the order and proposed compensated emancipation instead.

You cannot, if you would, be blind to the signs of the times. I beg of you a calm and enlarged consideration of them, ranging, if it may be, far above personal and partisan politics. This proposal makes common cause for a common object, casting no reproaches upon any. It acts not the Pharisee. The change it contemplates would come gently as the dews of heaven, not rending or wrecking anything. Will you not embrace it? So much good has not been done, by one effort, in all past time, as in the providence of God it is now your high privilege to do. May the vast future not have to lament that you have neglected it.

(NH VII, 172–73)

July 12, 1862
President Lincoln tried unsuccessfully to have Border State representatives accept a plan for gradual compensated emancipation.

If the war continues long, as it must if the object be not sooner attained, the institution in your states will be extinguished by mere friction and abrasion—by the mere incidents of the war. It will be gone, and you will have nothing valuable in lieu of it. Much of its value is gone already. How much better for you and for your people to take the step which at once shortens the war and secures substantial compensation for that which is sure to be wholly lost in any other event! How much better to thus save the money which else we sink forever in the war. How much better to do it while we can, lest the war ere long render us pecuniarily unable to do it! How much better for you as seller, and the nation as buyer, to sell out and buy out that without which the war could never have been, than to sink both the things to be sold and the price of it in cutting one another's throats? I do not speak of emancipation at once, but of a decision at once to emancipate gradually. Room in South America for colonization can be obtained cheaply and in abundance, and when numbers shall be large enough to be company and encouragement for one another, the freed people will not be so reluctant to go.

(NH VII, 272)

July 12, 1862
In the meeting with Border State representatives, Lincoln warned of mounting pressure by radical antislavery proponents.

General Hunter . . . proclaimed all men free within certain states, and I repudiated the proclamation. He expected more good and less harm from the measure than I could believe would follow. Yet, in repudiating it, I gave dissatisfaction, if not offense, to many whose support the country cannot afford to lose. And this is not the end of it. The pressure in this direction is still upon me, and is increasing.

(NH VII, 272–73)

July 22, 1862
Part of the preliminary draft of the Emancipation Proclamation submitted to Lincoln's Cabinet.

I, as commander-in-chief of the army and navy of the United States, do order and declare that on the first day of January, in the year of our Lord one thousand eight hundred and sixty-three, all persons held as slaves within any state or states wherein the constitutional authority of the United States shall not then be practically recognized, submitted to, and maintained, shall then, thence forward, and forever be free.

(NH VII, 290)

August 22, 1862
In an open letter to the editor of the New York Tribune, *Horace Greeley, Lincoln countered Greeley's opinion that slavery was the supreme issue in the ongoing war.*

My paramount object in this struggle is to save the Union, and is not either to save or to destroy slavery. If I could save the Union without freeing any slave, I would do it; and if I could save it by freeing all the slaves, I would do it; and if I could save it by freeing some and leaving others alone, I would also do that. What I do about slavery and the colored race, I do because I believe it helps to save the Union; and what I forbear, I forbear because I do not believe it would help to save the Union. I shall do less whenever I shall believe what I am doing hurts the cause, and I shall do more whenever I shall believe doing more will help the cause. I shall try to correct errors when shown to be errors, and I shall adopt new views so fast as they shall appear to be true views.

(NH VIII, 16)

September 13, 1862
To a committee of Christians who were in favor a proclamation of emancipation.

I admit that slavery is the root of the rebellion, or at least its sine qua non. The ambition of politicians may have instigated them to act, but they would have been impotent without slavery as their instrument. . . . I have not decided against a proclamation of liberty to the slaves, but hold the matter under advisement; and I can assure you that the subject is on my mind, by day and night, more than any other. Whatever shall appear to be God's will, I will do.

(NH VIII, 32–33)

September 22, 1862
When news of the Union victory at Antietam reached President
Lincoln, he decided to issue the Emancipation Proclamation.

That on the first day of January, in the year of our Lord one thousand eight hundred and sixty-three, all persons held as slaves within any state or designated part of a state the people whereof shall then be in rebellion against the United States, shall be then, thenceforward, and forever free; and the executive government of the United States, including the military and naval authority thereof, will recognize and maintain the freedom of such persons, and will do no act or acts to repress such persons, or any of them, in any efforts they make for their actual freedom.

(NH VIII, 37)

September 24, 1862
Response to a group of well-wishers gathered to celebrate the
Emancipation Proclamation.

What I did, I did after a very full deliberation, and under a very heavy and solemn sense of responsibility. I can only trust in God I have made no mistake.

(NH VIII, 44)

December 1, 1862
In his annual message to Congress, Lincoln remained cautiously
optimistic about the possibility of colonization.

Liberia and Haiti are as yet the only countries to which colonists of African descent from here could go with certainty of being received and adopted as citizens; and I regret to say such persons contemplating colonization do not seem so willing to migrate to those countries as to some others, nor so willing as I think their interest demands. I believe, however, opinion among them in this respect is improving; and that ere long there will be an augmented and considerable migration to both these countries from the United States.

(NH VIII, 97–98)

December 1, 1862
In his annual address, Lincoln presented his reasons for issuing the Emancipation Proclamation.

Among the friends of the Union there is great diversity of sentiment and of policy in regard to slavery and the African race among us. Some would perpetuate slavery; some would abolish it suddenly and without compensation; some would abolish it gradually, and with compensation; some would remove the freed people from us, and some would retain them with us; and there are yet other minor diversities. Because of these diversities we waste much strength in struggles among ourselves. By mutual concession we should harmonize and act together. This would be compromise; but it would be compromise among the friends, and not with the enemies of the Union. These articles are intended to embody a plan of such mutual concessions. If the plan shall be adopted, it is assumed that emancipation will follow at least in several of the states.

(NH VIII, 118)

December 1, 1862
President Lincoln's reply to opponents of the Emancipation Proclamation.

The dogmas of the quiet past are inadequate to the stormy present.

(NH VIII, 131)

January 1, 1863
The final version of the Emancipation Proclamation, which freed all slaves in the states still in rebellion and officially sanctioned the recruitment of African-Americans into the army and navy.

Now, therefore, I, Abraham Lincoln, President of the United States, by virtue of the power in me vested as commander-in-chief of the army and navy of the United States, in time of actual armed rebellion against the authority and government of the

United States, and as a fit and necessary war measure for suppressing said rebellion, do, on this first day of January, in the year of our Lord one thousand eight hundred and sixty-three, and in accordance with my purpose so to do, publicly proclaimed for the full period of 100 days from the day first mentioned, order and designate as the states and parts of states wherein the people thereof, respectively, are this day in rebellion against the United States, the following, to wit:

Arkansas, Texas, Louisiana (except the parishes of St. Bernard, Plaquemines, Jefferson, St. John, St. Charles, St. James, Ascension, Assumption, Terre Bonne, Lafourche, St. Mary, St. Martin, and Orleans, including the city of New Orleans), Mississippi, Alabama, Florida, Georgia, South Carolina, North Carolina, and Virginia (except the forty-eight counties designated as West Virginia, and also the counties of Berkeley, Accomac, Northampton, Elizabeth City, York, Princess Anne, and Norfolk, including the cities of Norfolk and Portsmouth), and which excepted parts are for the present left precisely as if this proclamation were not issued.

And by virtue of the power and for the purpose aforesaid, I do order and declare that all persons held as slaves within said designated states and parts of states are, and henceforward shall be, free; and that the executive government of the United States, including the military and naval authorities thereof, will recognize and maintain the freedom of said persons.

And I hereby enjoin upon the people so declared to be free to abstain from all violence, unless in necessary self defense; and I recommend to them that, in all cases where allowed, they labor faithfully for reasonable wages.

And I further declare and make known that such persons of suitable condition will be received into the armed service of the United States to garrison forts, positions, stations, and other places, and to man vessels of all sorts in said service.

And upon this act, sincerely believed to be an act of justice, warranted by the Constitution upon military necessity, I invoke the considerate judgment of mankind and the gracious favor of Almighty God.

(NH VIII, 161–64)

August 26, 1863
Lincoln's rationale for giving freedom to African-Americans who fought in the Civil War.

I thought that whatever negroes can be got to do as soldiers, leaves just so much less for white soldiers to do in saving the Union. . . . But negroes, like other people, act upon motives. Why should they, do anything for us if we will do nothing for them? If they stake their lives for us they must be prompted by the strongest motive, even the promise of freedom. And the promise, being made, must be kept.

(NH IX, 100)

March 13, 1864
Letter to the new governor of the reorganized state of Louisiana.

Now you are about to have a convention, which, among other things, will probably define the elective franchise. I barely suggest for your private consideration, whether some of the colored people may not be let in—as, for instance, the very intelligent, and especially those who have fought gallantly in our ranks. They would probably help, in some trying time to come, to keep the jewel of liberty within the family of freedom. But this is only a suggestion, not to the public, but to you alone.

(NH X, 38–39)

April 4, 1864
An account by President Lincoln of his conversation with the pro-Union governor of Kentucky.

I am naturally antislavery. If slavery is not wrong, nothing is wrong. I cannot remember when I did not so think and feel, and yet I have never understood that the presidency conferred upon me an unrestricted right to act officially upon this judgment and feeling.

(NH X, 65)

April 4, 1864
An account of the progress from enslavement to emancipation, as described to the governor of Kentucky.

When General Fremont attempted military emancipation, I forbade it, because I did not then think it an indispensable necessity. When, a little later, General Cameron, then Secretary of War, suggested the arming of the blacks, I objected because I did not yet think it an indispensable necessity. When, still later, General Hunter attempted military emancipation, I again forbade it, because I did not yet think the indispensable necessity had come. When in March and May and July, 1862, I made earnest and successive appeals to the border states to favor compensated emancipation, I believed the indispensable necessity for military emancipation and arming the blacks would come unless averted by that measure. They declined the proposition, and I was, in my best judgment, driven to the alternative of either surrendering the Union, and with it the Constitution, or of laying strong hand upon the colored element. I chose the latter. In choosing it, I hoped for greater gain than loss; but of this, I was not entirely confident. More than a year of trial now shows no loss by it in our foreign relations, none in our home popular sentiment, none in our while military force—no loss by it anyhow or anywhere. On the contrary it shows a gain of quite a hundred and thirty thousand soldiers, seamen, and laborers. These are palpable facts, about which, as facts, there can be no caviling. We have the men; and we could not have had them without the measure.

(NH X, 66–67)

April 15, 1864
President Lincoln received a petition from schoolchildren asking that all enslaved children be freed.

Please tell these little people I am very glad their young hearts are so full of just and generous sympathy, and that, while I have not the power to grant all they ask, I trust they will remember that God has, and that, as it seems, he wills to do it.

(NH X, 68–69)

May 30, 1864
From a letter to members of the American Baptist Home Mission Society, regarding the institution of slavery.

When brought to my final reckoning, may I have to answer for robbing no man of his goods yet more tolerable even this, that for robbing one of himself and all that was his. When, a year or two ago, those professedly holy men of the South met in semblance of prayer and devotion, and, in the name of him who said, "As ye would all men should do unto you, do ye even so unto them," appealed to the Christian world to aid them in doing to a whole race of men as they would have no man do unto themselves, to my thinking they contemned and insulted God and his church far more than did Satan when he tempted the Savior with the kingdoms of the earth. The devil's attempt was no more false, and far less hypocritical. But let me forbear, remembering it is also written, "Judge not lest ye be judged."

(NH X, 110)

September 7, 1864
Remarks made when Lincoln was presented with a Bible by a visiting group of African-Americans.

I can only now say, as I have often before said, it has always been a sentiment with me that all mankind should be free. So far as able, within my sphere, I have always acted as I believe to be right and

just; and I have done all I could for the good of mankind generally.

(NH X, 217–18)

December 6, 1864
Lincoln solicited Congressional support for the Thirteenth Amend-
ment in his annual message to Congress.

At the last session of Congress a proposed amendment of the
Constitution, abolishing slavery throughout the United States,
passed the Senate, but failed for lack of the requisite two-thirds
vote in the House of Representatives. Although the present is the
same Congress, and nearly the same members, and without ques-
tioning the wisdom or patriotism of those who stood in opposition, I venture to recommend the reconsideration and passage of
the measure at the present session. Of course the abstract question
is not changed, but an intervening election shows, almost certainly, that the next Congress will pass the measure if this does
not. Hence there is only a question of time as to when the proposed amendment will go to the states for their action. And as it
is to so go, at all events, may we not agree that the sooner the better?

(NH X, 303–04)

January 31, 1865
Response to a group of well-wishers on the day that the Thirteenth
Amendment was presented to the House of Representatives. The
amendment was ratified on December 18, 1865, seven months
after Lincoln's death.

This amendment is a king's cure-all for all evils. It winds the
whole thing up. He would repeat that it was the fitting if not the
indispensable adjunct to the consummation of the great game we
are playing. He could not but congratulate all present—himself,
the country, and the whole world—upon this great moral victory.

(NH X, 353)

PART IV

Private Life

Tall, rail thin and unkempt in appearance, the young Abraham Lincoln was a lonely, self conscious young man and inept around girls. To make matters worse, he was prone to severe bouts of depression, as happened when his engagement with Mary Todd was broken off. Though he doubted the wisdom of his decision, he nevertheless married Mary Todd and settled into a reasonably happy married life. Four sons were born, but only the oldest, Robert Todd, survived to adulthood. Lincoln was a complicated man who, though he did not subscribe to any particular religion, could quote the Bible extensively and believed in Providence. He believed in reason, but was superstitious about his dreams. He took delight in telling jokes, but brooded often upon the subject of death.

December 13, 1836
Lincoln was very shy and awkward with girls, as he revealed in this letter to Mary Owens, whom he was courting.

I have been sick ever since my arrival here, or I should have written sooner. It is but little difference, however, as I have very little even yet to write. And more, the longer I can avoid the mortification of looking in the post office for your letter and not finding it, the better. You see I am mad about that old letter yet. I don't like very well to risk you again. I'll try you once more any how. . . .
You recollect that I mentioned at the outset of this letter that I had been unwell. That is the fact, though I believe I am about well now; but that, with other things I cannot account for, have con-

spired and have gotten my spirits so low that I feel that I would rather be any placc in thc world than here. I really cannot endure the thought of staying here ten weeks. Write back as soon as you get this, and if possible say something that will please me, for really I have not been pleased since I left you. This letter is so dry and stupid that I am ashamed to send it, but with my present feelings I cannot do any better.

(CW I, 54–55)

May 7, 1837
In another letter to Mary Owens, Lincoln related his feelings of loneliness and hinted that she might be better off without him.

I have commenced two letters to send you before this, both of which displeased me before I got half done, and so I tore them up. The first I thought wasn't serious enough, and the second was on the other extreme. I shall send this, turn out as it may.

This thing of living in Springfield is rather a dull business after all, at least it is to me. I am quite as lonesome here as I ever was anywhere in my life. I have been spoken to by but one woman since I've been here, and should not have been by her if she could have avoided it. I've never been to church yet, and probably shall not be soon. I stay away because I am conscious I should not know how to behave myself.

I am often thinking about what we said of your coming to live at Springfield. I am afraid you would not be satisfied. There is a great deal of flourishing about in carriages here, which it would be your doom to see without sharing it. You would have to be poor without the means of hiding your poverty. Do you believe you could bear that patiently? Whatever woman may cast her lot with mine, should any ever do so, it is my intention to do all in my power to make her happy and contented; and there is nothing I can imagine, that would make me more unhappy than to fail in the effort.

(CW I, 78)

August 16, 1837
From Lincoln's last letter to Mary Owens, to which there was no
reply.

I want in all cases to do right, and most particularly so, in all cases
with women. I want, at this particular time, more than anything
else, to do right with you, and if I *knew* it would be doing right, as
I rather suspect it would, to let you alone, I would do it. And for
the purpose of making the matter as plain as possible, I now say,
that you can now drop the subject, dismiss your thoughts (if you
ever had any) from me forever, and leave this letter unanswered,
without calling forth one accusing murmur from me. And I will
even go further, and say, that if it will add anything to your comfort, or peace of mind, to do so, it is my sincere wish that you
should. Do not understand by this, that I wish to cut your acquaintance. I mean no such thing. What I do wish is, that our further acquaintance shall depend upon yourself. If such further
acquaintance would contribute nothing to your happiness, I am
sure it would not to mine. If you feel yourself in any degree bound
to me, I am now willing to release you, provided you wish it;
while, on the other hand, I am willing, and even anxious to bind
you faster, if I can be convinced that it will, in any considerable
degree, add to your happiness. This, indeed, is the whole question
with me. Nothing would make me more miserable than to believe
you miserable—nothing more happy, than to know you were so.

(CW I, 94)

April 1, 1838
To Mrs. O. H. Browning, in which he described the termination
of his relationship with Mary Owens.

I finally was forced to give it up, at which I very unexpectedly
found myself mortified almost beyond endurance. I was mortified,
it seemed to me, in a hundred different ways. My vanity was
deeply wounded by the reflection that I had so long been too stupid to discover her intentions, and at the same time never doubt-

ing that I understood them perfectly; and also that she, whom I had taught myself to believe nobody else would have, had actually rejected me with all my fancied greatness; and to cap the whole, I then, for the first time began to suspect that I was really a little in love with her. But let it all go. I'll try and outlive it. Others have been made fools of by the girls; but this can never be with truth said of me. I most emphatically, in this instance, made a fool of myself. I have now come to the conclusion never again to think of marrying; and for this reason; I can never be satisfied with anyone who would be blockhead enough to have me.

(CW I, 119)

January 20, 1841
Letter telling of Lincoln's bout with depression after the broken
engagement with Mary Todd on January 1, 1841.

I have, within the last few days, been making a most discreditable exhibition of myself in the way of hypochondriaism and thereby got an impression that Dr. Henry is necessary to my existence. . . . Pardon me for not writing more; I have not sufficient composure to write a long letter.

(CW I, 228)

January 23, 1841
In another letter regarding the broken engagement with Mary
Todd, Lincoln described his deep sadness.

I am now the most miserable man living. If what I feel were equally distributed to the whole human family, there would not be one cheerful face on the earth. Whether I shall ever be better, I cannot tell; I awfully forebode I shall not. To remain as I am is impossible; I must die or be better, it appears to me.

(NH I, 159)

February 3, 1842
Lincoln wrote to assure his friend, Joshua Speed, that his depression was finally lifting.

You know the hell I have suffered on that point, and how tender I am upon it. You know I do mean no wrong. I have been quite clear of "hypo" since you left; even better than I was along in the fall.

(NH I, 187)

February 22, 1842
Lincoln on telling the truth.

I never encourage deceit, and falsehood, especially if you have got a bad memory, is the worst enemy a fellow can have. The fact is truth is your truest friend, no matter what the circumstances are.

(NH I, 191)

February 22, 1842
Lincoln, who did not drink, was a moderate compared to many in the temperance movement.

The warfare heretofore waged against the demon intemperance has somehow or other been erroneous. Either the champions engaged or the tactics they adopted have not been the most proper. These champions for the most part have been preachers, lawyers, and hired agents. Between these and the mass of mankind there is a want of approachability. . . . Too much denunciation against dram-sellers and dram-drinkers was indulged in. This I think was impolitic, because it is not much in the nature of man to be driven to anything; still less to be driven about that which is exclusively his own business; and least of all where such driving is to be submitted to at the expense of the pecuniary interest or burning appetite.

(NH I, 194–96)

February 22, 1842
Address to Springfield's Washington Temperance Society.

When the conduct of men is designed to be influenced, persuasion—kind, unassuming persuasion—should ever be adopted. It is an old and a true maxim that "a drop of honey catches more flies than a gallon of gall." So with men. If you would win a man to your cause, first convince him that you are his sincere friend. Therein is a drop of honey that catches his heart, which, say what he will, is the great highroad to his reason, and which, when once gained, you will find but little trouble in convincing his judgment of the justice of your cause, if indeed that cause really be a just one. On the contrary, assume to dictate to his judgment, or to command his action, or to mark him as one to be shunned and despised, and he will retreat within himself, close all the avenues to his head and his heart; and though your cause be naked truth itself, transformed to the heaviest lance, harder than steel, and sharper than steel can be made, and though you throw it with more than Herculean force and precision, you shall be no more able to pierce him than to penetrate the hard shell of a tortoise with a rye straw. Such is man, and so much he be understood by those who would lead him, even to his own best interests.

(NH I, 197)

February 25, 1842
Upon finding out that Joshua Speed could not come to Illinois for a visit.

I shall be very lonesome without you. How miserably things seem to be arranged in this world! If we have no friends, we have no pleasure; and if we have them, we are sure to lose them, and be doubly pained by the loss.

(NH I, 210)

July 4, 1842
Another account of the pain caused by the broken engagement
with Mary Todd. Lincoln married her four months later.

I acknowledge the correctness of your advice too; but before I resolve to do the one thing or the other, I must regain my confidence in my own ability to keep my resolves when they are made.
In that ability, you know, I once prided myself as the only, or at
least the chief, gem of my character; that gem I lost—how, and
when, you too well know. I have not yet regained it; and until I do,
I can not trust myself in any matter of much importance.

(CW I, 289)

September 19, 1842
In late August, 1842, Lincoln penned a pseudonymous letter
(signed "Rebecca") to the Sangamo Journal, *in which he ridiculed*
a Democratic politician, James Shields. Shields, upon learning
that Lincoln was the author, challenged Lincoln to a duel, and ac-
cording to the rules of engagement, Lincoln had to decide on the
weapons, a choice shaped by the physical advantage over his oppo-
nent, who was considerably shorter in height. Dueling was illegal
in Illinois, so the fight was scheduled to take place across the river
in Missouri. The duel was avoided when Lincoln proclaimed that
he had not intentionally sought to injure Shields' reputation.

The preliminaries of the fight are to be—
    1st. Weapons—Cavalry broad swords of the largest size, pre-
cisely equal in all respects—and such as now are used by the cav-
alry company at Jacksonville.
    2nd. Position—A plank ten feet long, and from nine to twelve
inches broad to be firmly fixed on edge, on the ground, as the line
between us which neither is to pass his foot over upon forfeit of
his life. Next a line drawn on the ground on either side of said
plank and parallel with it, each at the distance of the whole length
of the sword and three feet additional from the plank; and the

passing of his own such line by either party during the fight shall be deemed a surrender of the contest.

3d. Time—On Thursday evening at five o'clock if you can get it so; but in no case to be at a greater distance of time than Friday evening at five o'clock.

4th. Place—Within three miles of Alton on the opposite side of the river, the particular spot to be agreed on by you.

(CW I, 301)

October 5, 1842
Nervous about his impending marriage to Mary Todd, Lincoln wrote his friend, Joshua Speed, who had also been hesitant to marry, for support. Lincoln married Mary Todd one month later, on November 4, 1842.

The immense suffering you endured from the first days of September till the middle of February you never tried to conceal from me, and I well understood. You have now been the husband of a lovely woman nearly eight months. That you are happier now than you were the day you married her I well know; for without, you would not be living. But I have your word for it too; and the returning elasticity of spirits which is manifested in your letters. But I want to ask a closer question—"Are you now, in feeling as well as judgment, glad you are married as you are?" From anybody but me, this would be an impudent question not to be tolerated; but I know you will pardon it in me. Please answer it quickly as I feel impatient to know.

(CW I, 303)

February 25, 1846
Lincoln published one poem during his life, which he explained as resulting from a visit to his boyhood home in Indiana in 1844. Its subject—madness—was likely connected to Lincoln's fears concerning his own mental stability.

Near twenty years have passed away
    Since here I bid farewell

To woods, and fields, and scenes of play
    And school-mates loved so well.

Where many were, how few remain
    Of old familiar things!
But seeing them, to mind again
    The lost and absent brings.

The friends I left that parting day—
    How changed, as time has sped!
Young childhood grown, strong manhood gray,
    And half of all are dead.

I hear the loved survivors tell
    How naught from death could save,
Till every sound appears a knell,
    And every spot a grave.

I range the fields with pensive tread,
    And pace the hollow rooms;
And feel (companion of the dead)
    I'm living in the tombs.

And here's an object more of dread,
    Than ought the grave contains—
A human-form, with reason fled,
    While wretched life remains.

Poor Matthew! Once of genius bright,—
    A fortune-favored child—
Now locked for aye, in mental night,
    A haggard mad-man wild.

Poor Matthew! I have ne'er forgot
    When first with maddened will,
Yourself you maimed, your father fought,
    And mother strove to kill;

And terror spread, and neighbors ran,
    Your dang'rous strength to bind;
And soon a howling crazy man,
    Your limbs were fast confined.

How then you writhed and shrieked aloud,
    Your bones and sinews bared;
And fiendish on the gaping crowd,
    With burning eye-balls glared.

And begged, and swore, and wept, and prayed,
    With maniac laughter joined—
How fearful are the signs displayed,
    By pangs that kill the mind!

And when at length, tho' drear and long,
    Time soothed your fiercer woes—
How plaintively your mournful song,
    Upon the still night rose.

I've heard it oft, as if I dreamed,
    Far distant, sweet, and lone;
The funeral dirge it ever seemed
    Of reason dead and gone. . . .

                      (CW I, 367–9)

July 31, 1846
During his campaign for Congress, Lincoln wrote to the Illinois
Gazette *to answer accusations that he was irreligious.*

That I am not a member of any Christian church is true; but I
have never denied the truth of the Scriptures; and I have never
spoken with intentional disrespect of religion in general, or of any
denomination of Christians in particular. It is true that in early
life I was inclined to believe in what I understand is called the
"Doctrine of Necessity"—that is, that the human mind is im-
pelled to action, or held in rest by some power, over which the

mind itself has not control; and I have sometimes (with one, two or three, but never publicly) tried to maintain this opinion in argument. The habit of arguing thus however, I have, entirely left off for more than five years. . . .

I do not think I could myself, be brought to support a man for office, whom I knew to be an open enemy of, and scoffer at, religion. Leaving the higher matter of eternal consequences, between him and his Maker, I still do not think any man has the right thus to insult the feelings, and injure the morals, of the community in which he may live. If, then, I was guilty of such conduct, I should blame no man who should condemn me for it; but I do blame those, whoever they may be, who falsely put such a charge in circulation against me.

(CW I, 382)

August 11, 1846
In another letter to the Illinois Gazette, *Lincoln answered an attack from a Democratic opponent.*

There is . . . one lesson in morals which he might, not without profit, learn of even me—and that is, never to add the weight of his character to a charge against his fellow man, without knowing it to be true. I believe it is an established maxim in morals that he who makes an assertion without knowing whether it is true or false, is guilty of falsehood; and the accidental truth of the assertion, does not justify or excuse him. This maxim ought to be particularly held in view, when we contemplate an attack upon the reputation of our neighbor.

(CW I, 383–84)

October 22, 1846
Mary Todd Lincoln gave birth to their first son Robert (Bob) Todd Lincoln on August 1, 1843. Edward (Eddy) Baker was seven months old at the time this letter was written.

We have another boy, born the 10th of March. He is very much such a child as Bob was at his age, rather of a longer order. Bob is "short and low," and I expect always will be. He talks very plainly—almost as plainly as anybody. He is quite smart enough. I sometimes fear that he is one of the little rare-ripe sort that are smarter at about five than ever after. He has a great deal of that sort of mischief that is the offspring of such animal spirits. Since I began this letter, a messenger came to tell me Bob was lost; but by the time I reached the house his mother had found him and had him whipped, and by now, very likely, he is run away again.

(NH I, 298)

April 16, 1848
When Lincoln was elected to the House of Representatives, he longed for his wife and children to join him in Washington.

In this troublesome world, we are never quite satisfied. When you were here, I thought you hindered me some in attending to business; but now, having nothing but business—no variety—it has grown exceedingly tasteless to me. I hate to sit down and direct documents, and I hate to stay in this old room by myself. . . .

And are you entirely free from headache? That is good—good—considering it is the first spring you have been free from it since we were acquainted. I am afraid you will get so well, and fat, and young, as to be wanting to marry again. Tell Louisa I want her to watch you a little for me. Get weighed, and write me how much you weigh.

(CW I, 465–66)

June 12, 1848
A letter to Mary Todd Lincoln, written while the House of Representatives was in session.

On my return from Philadelphia yesterday, where, in my anxiety I had been led to attend the Whig convention, I found your last letter. I was so tired and sleepy, having ridden all night, that I could not answer it till today; and now I have to do so in the H. R. The leading matter in your letter is your wish to return to this side of the mountains. Will you be a good girl in all things, if I consent? Then come along, and that as soon as possible. Having got the idea in my head, I shall be impatient till I see you. . . . Come on just as soon as you can. I want to see you, and our dear, dear boys very much.

(CW I, 477–78)

July 2, 1848
Washington gossip communicated to Mary Todd Lincoln, who was at home in Illinois.

Our two girls, whom you remember seeing first at Carusis [Saloon], at the exhibition of the Ethiopian Serenaders, and whose peculiarities were the wearing of black fur bonnets, and never being seen in close company with other ladies, were at the music yesterday. One of them was attended by their brother, and the other had a member of Congress in tow. He went home with her; and if I were to guess, I would say, he went away a somewhat altered man—most likely in his pockets, and in some other particular. The fellow looked conscious of guilt, although I believe he was unconscious that everybody around knew who it was that had caught him . . .

By the way, you do not intend to do without a girl, because the one you had has left you? Get another as soon as you can to take charge of the dear codgers. Father expected to see you all sooner; but let it pass; stay as long as you please, and come when you please. Kiss and love the dear rascals.

(CW I, 495–96)

July 10, 1848
Letter of advice to his law partner and friend, William Herndon, who was convinced that some influential men in the community were preventing his success.

The way for a young man to rise, is to improve himself every way he can, never suspecting that anybody wishes to hinder him. Allow me to assure you, that suspicion and jealousy never did help any man in any situation. There may sometimes be ungenerous attempts to keep a young man down; and they will succeed, too, if he allows his mind to be diverted from its true channel to brood over the attempted injury. Cast about, and see if this feeling has not injured every person you have ever known to fall into it. . . . You can not fail in any laudable object, unless you allow your mind to be improperly directed. I have some the advantage of you in the world's experience, merely by being older; and it is this that induces me to advise.

(CW I, 497–98)

December 24, 1849
A letter to Lincoln's foster brother, John Johnston, who had asked for money.

You are not lazy, and still you are an idler. I doubt whether, since I saw you, you have done a good whole day's work, in any one day. You do not very much dislike to work; and still you do not work much, merely because it does not seem to you that you could get much for it. This habit of uselessly wasting time, is the whole difficulty; and it is vastly important to you, and still more so to your children that you should break the habit. It is more important to them, because they have longer to live, and can keep out of an idle habit before they are in it; easier than they can get out after they are in.

(CW II, 16)

February 23, 1850
Lincoln's youngest son, Edward (Eddie) Baker Lincoln, died from pulmonary tuberculosis on February 1, 1850, shortly before he reached the age of four.

As you make no mention of it, I suppose you had not learned that we lost our little boy. He was sick fifty-two days, and died in the morning of the first day of this month. It was not our first, but our second child. We miss him very much.

(NH II, 135)

January 12, 1851
Lincoln learned that his father was ill shortly after Mary Todd Lincoln gave birth to another son, William (Willie) Wallace Lincoln, on December 21, 1850. Lincoln's father died on January 17, 1851.

You already know I desire that neither father or mother shall be in want of any comfort either in health or sickness while they live; and I feel sure you have not failed to use my name, if necessary, to procure a doctor, or anything else for father in his present sickness. My business is such that I could hardly leave home now, if it was not as it is, that my own wife is sick-abed. (It is a case of baby-sickness, and I suppose is not dangerous.) I sincerely hope father may recover his health, but at all events, tell him to remember to call upon and confide in our great and good and merciful Maker, who will not turn away from him in any extremity. He notes the fall of a sparrow, and numbers the hairs of our heads, and He will not forget the dying man who puts his trust in Him. Say to him that if we could meet now it is doubtful whether it would not be more painful than pleasant, but that if it be his lot to go now, he will soon have a joyous meeting with many loved ones gone before, and where the rest of us, through the help of God, hope ere long to join them.

(CW II, 96–97)

November 4, 1851
Another letter to Lincoln's foster brother, John Johnston, who considered selling his farm and moving to Missouri.

I have been thinking of this ever since, and cannot but think such a notion is utterly foolish. What can you do in Missouri better than here? Is the land any richer? Can you there, any more than here, raise corn and wheat and oats without work? Will anybody there, any more than here, do your work for you? If you intend to go to work, there is no better place than right where you are; if you do not intend to go to work, you cannot get along anywhere.

Squirming and crawling about from place to place can do no good.

(NH II, 150)

March 31, 1854
Biographical details supplied to a distant relative.

As you have supposed, I am the grandson of your uncle Abraham; and the story of his death by the Indians, and of Uncle Mordecai, then fourteen years old, killing one of the Indians, is the legend more strongly than all others imprinted upon my mind and memory. . . . My father (Thomas) died the 17th of January, 1851, in Coles County, Illinois, where he had resided twenty years. I am his only child. I have resided here, and hereabouts, twenty-three years. I am forty-five years of age, and have a wife and three children, the oldest eleven years. My wife was born and raised at Lexington, Kentucky; and my connection with her has sometimes taken me there, where I have heard the older people of her relations speak of your uncle Thomas and his family. . . . I can no longer claim to be a young man myself; but I infer that, as you are of the same generation as my father, you are some older.

(CW II, 217–18)

July 25, 1858
Lincoln was fascinated by the subject of death, as expressed here in his eulogy for President Zachary Taylor.

The death of the late president may not be without its use, in reminding us, that we too, must die. Death, abstractly considered, is the same with the high as with the low; but practically, we are not so much aroused to the contemplation of our own mortal natures, by the fall of many undistinguished, as that of one great, and well known, name. By the latter, we are forced to muse, and ponder, sadly.

(CW II, 90)

November 16, 1858
Lincoln accrued some debts during his failed bid for the Senate.

As to the pecuniary matter, I am willing to pay according to my ability; but I am the poorest hand living to get others to pay. I have been on expenses so long without earning anything that I am absolutely without money now for even household purposes. Still, if you can put in two hundred and fifty dollars for me towards discharging the debt of the Committee, I will allow it when you and I settle the private matter between us.

(CW III, 337)

September 30, 1859
From a speech to the Wisconsin State Agricultural Association.

Constituted as man is, he has positive need of occasional recreation, and whatever can give him this associated with virtue and advantage, and free from vice and disadvantage, is a positive good.

(NH V, 237)

March 4, 1860
Note to Mary Lincoln, two months before Lincoln became the Republican candidate for president.

I have been unable to escape this toil. If I had foreseen it, I think I would not have come east at all.

(CW III, 555)

June 1, 1860
A story from childhood, provided for a biographical pamphlet during the presidential election of 1860.

A few days before the completion of his eighth year, in the absence of his father, a flock of wild turkeys approached the new log cabin, and Abraham with a rifle, standing inside, shot through a crack and killed one of them. He has never since pulled a trigger on any larger game.

(NH VI, 27)

July 4, 1860
A description of Lincoln's sons, Robert (Bob) and William (Willie), from a letter to a friend.

Our boy, in his tenth year (the baby when you left), has just had a hard and tedious spell of scarlet fever, and he is not yet beyond all danger. . . . Our eldest boy, Bob, has been away from us nearly a year at school, and will enter Harvard University this month. He promises well, considering we never controlled him much.

(NH VI, 43)

August 31, 1860
Letter to a friend who had written to congratulate Lincoln on his nomination for the presidency.

How time gallops along with us! Look at these great big boys of yours and mine, when it is but yesterday that we and their mothers were unmarried.

(CW IV, 103)

June 9, 1863
Lincoln believed that some of his dreams were premonitions, as in this telegram to Mary Todd Lincoln.

Think you had better put Tad's pistol away. I had an ugly dream about him.

(NH VIII, 296)

July 3, 1863
Telegram advising son Robert of his mother's condition after she fell from a carriage.

Don't be uneasy. Your mother very slightly hurt by her fall.

(NH IX, 15)

August 8, 1863
Letter to Mary Todd Lincoln, on the goat kept at the White
House for his son Thomas (Tad).

Tell dear Tad poor "Nanny Goat" is lost, and Mrs. Cuthbert and I
are in distress about it. The day you left, Nanny was found resting
herself and chewing her little cud on the middle of Tad's bed; but
now she's gone! The gardener kept complaining that she destroyed the flowers, till it was concluded to bring her down to the
White House. This was done, and the second day she had disap-
peared and has not been heard of since. This is the last we know of
poor "Nanny."

(NH IX, 61–62)

September 29, 1863
From a reply to the Sons of Intemperance.

I think that the reasonable men of the world have long since
agreed that intemperance is one of the greatest, if not the very
greatest, of all evils among mankind.

(NH IX, 145)

June 24, 1864
Telegram to Mary Todd Lincoln, reassuring her after he and son
Thomas (Tad) made a visit to General Ulysses S. Grant's head-
quarters at City Point, Virginia.

All well and very warm. Tad and I have been to General Grant's
army. Returned yesterday safe and sound.

(NH X, 134)

January 19, 1865
Lincoln wrote General Grant to inquire whether his son Robert
(Bob) could spend some time on Grant's staff.

My son, now in his twenty-second year, having graduated from
Harvard, wishes to see something of the war before it ends. I do

not wish to put him in the ranks, nor yet to give him a commission, to which those who have already served long are better entitled and better qualified to hold. Could he, without embarrassment to you or detriment to the service, go into your military family with some nominal rank, I, and not the public, furnishing his necessary means? If no, say so without the least hesitation, because I am as anxious and as deeply interested that you shall not be encumbered as you can be yourself.

(NH X, 343)

April 2, 1865
Lincoln and his son Thomas (Tad) visited City Point, Virginia, while General Grant was attacking Petersburg. Telegrams were sent to Mary Todd Lincoln to keep her abreast of their travels and assure her of their safety.

At 4:30 P.M. today General Grant telegraphs that he has Petersburg completely enveloped from river below to river above, and has captured since he started last Wednesday, about 12,000 prisoners and 50 guns. He suggests that I shall go out and see him in the morning, which I think I will do. Tad and I are both well, and will be glad to see you and your party here at the time you name.

(NH XI, 67)

Appendixes

Young Men's Lyceum Address

January 27, 1838
Lincoln's first major speech, in which he touched on the major themes that he would return to throughout his political career.

As a subject for the remarks of the evening, "The perpetuation of our political institutions" is selected.

In the great journal of things happening under the sun, we, the American people, find our account running under the date of the nineteenth century of the Christian era. We find ourselves in the peaceful possession of the fairest portion of the earth as regards extent of territory, fertility of soil, and salubrity of climate. We find ourselves under the government of a system of political institutions conducing more essentially to the ends of civil and religious liberty than any of which the history of former times tells us. We, when mounting the stage of existence, found ourselves the legal inheritors of these fundamental blessings. We toiled not in the acquirement or establishment of them; they are a legacy bequeathed us by a once hardy, brave, and patriotic, but now lamented and departed, race of ancestors. Theirs was the task (and nobly they performed it) to possess themselves, and through themselves us, of this goodly land, and to uprear upon its hills and its valleys a political edifice of liberty and equal rights; 'tis ours only to transmit these—the former unprofaned by the foot of an invader, the latter undecayed by the lapse of time and untorn by usurpation—to the latest generation that fate shall permit the world to know. This task of gratitude to our fathers, justice to ourselves, duty to posterity, and love for our species in general, all imperatively require us faithfully to perform.

How then shall we perform it? At what point shall we expect the approach of danger? By what means shall we fortify against it? Shall we expect some transatlantic military giant to step the ocean and crush us at a blow? Never! All the armies of Europe, Asia, and Africa combined, with all the treasure of the earth (our own excepted) in their military chest, with a Bonaparte for a commander, could not by force take a drink from the Ohio or make a track on the Blue Ridge in a trial of a thousand years.

At what point, then, is the approach of danger to be expected? I answer, If it ever reach us it must spring up amongst us; it cannot come from abroad. If destruction be our lot we must ourselves be its author and finisher. As a nation of freemen we must live through all time, or die by suicide.

I hope I am over wary; but if I am not, there is even now something of ill omen amongst us. I mean the increasing disregard for law which pervades the country—the growing disposition to substitute the wild and furious passions in lieu of the sober judgment of courts, and the worse than savage mobs for the executive ministers of justice. This disposition is awfully fearful in any community; and that it now exists in ours, though grating to our feelings to admit, it would be a violation of truth and an insult to our intelligence to deny. Accounts of outrages committed by mobs form the everyday news of the times. They have pervaded the country from New England to Louisiana; they are neither peculiar to the eternal snows of the former nor the burning suns of the latter; they are not the creature of climate, neither are they confined to the slaveholding or the non-slaveholding states. Alike they spring up among the pleasure-hunting masters of Southern slaves, and the order-loving citizens of the land of steady habits. Whatever then their cause may be, it is common to the whole country.

It would be tedious as well as useless to recount the horrors of all of them. Those happening in the state of Mississippi and at St. Louis are perhaps the most dangerous in example and revolting to humanity. In the Mississippi case they first commenced by hanging the regular gamblers—a set of men certainly not following for a livelihood a very useful or very honest occupation, but one which, so far from being forbidden by the laws, was actually licensed by an act of the legislature passed but a single year before. Next, negroes suspected of conspiring to raise an insurrection were caught up and hanged in all parts of the state; then, white men supposed to be leagued with the negroes; and finally, strangers from the neighboring states, going thither on business, were in many instances subjected to the same fate. Thus went on this process of hanging, from gamblers to negroes, from negroes to white citizens, and from these to strangers, till dead men were seen literally dangling from the boughs of trees upon every roadside, and in numbers almost sufficient to rival the Spanish moss of the country as a drapery of the forest.

Turn, then, to that horror-striking scene at St. Louis. A single victim was sacrificed there. This story is very short, and is perhaps the most highly tragic of anything of its length that has ever been witnesses in real life. A mulatto man by the name of McIntosh was seized in the street, dragged to the suburbs of the city, chained to a tree, and actually burned to death; and all within a single hour from the time he had been a freeman attending to his own business and at peace with the world.

Such are the effects of mob law, and such are the scenes becoming more and more frequent in this land so lately famed for love of law and order, and the stories of which have even now grown too familiar to attract anything more than an idle remark.

But you are perhaps ready to ask, "What has this to do with the perpetuation of our political institutions?" I answer, "It has much to do with it." Its direct consequences are, comparatively speaking, but a small evil, and much of its danger consists in the proneness of our minds to regard its direct as its only consequences. Abstractly considered, the hanging of the gamblers at Vicksburg was of but little consequence. They constitute a portion of population that is worse than useless in any community; and their death, if no perni-

cious example be set by it, is never a matter of reasonable regret
with anyone. If they were annually swept from the stage of existence by the plague or smallpox, honest men would perhaps be
much profited by the operation. Similar, too, is the correct reasoning in regard to the burning of the negro in St. Louis. He had forfeited his life by the perpetration of an outrageous murder upon
one of the most worthy and respectable citizens of the city, and
had he not died as he did, he must have died by the sentence of
the law in a very short time afterward. As to him alone, it was as
well the way it was as it could otherwise have been. But the example in either case was fearful. When men take it in their heads
today to hang gamblers or burn murderers, they should recollect
that in the confusion usually attending such transactions they will
be as likely to hang or burn someone who is neither a gambler nor
a murderer as one who is, and that, acting upon the example they
set, the mob of tomorrow may, and probably will, nag or burn
some of them by the very same mistake. And not only so; the innocent, those who have ever set their faces against violations of
law in every shape, alike with the guilty fall victims to the ravages
of mob law; and thus it goes up, step by step, till all the walls
erected for the defense of the persons and property of individuals
are trodden down and disregarded. But all this, even, is not the
full extent of the evil. By such examples, by instances of the per-
petrators of such acts going unpunished, the lawless in spirit are
encouraged to become lawless in practice; and having been used
to no restraint but dread of punishment, they thus become absolutely unrestrained. Having ever regarded government as their
deadliest bane, they make a jubilee of the suspension of its operations, and pray for nothing so much as its total annihilation.
While, on the other hand, good men, men who love tranquility,
who desire to abide by the laws and enjoy their benefits, who
would gladly spill their blood in the defense of their country, seeing their property destroyed, their families insulted, and their lives
endangered, their persons injured, and seeing nothing in prospect
that forebodes a change for the better, become tired of and dis-

gusted with a government that offers them no protection, and are not much averse to a change in which they imagine that they have nothing to lose. Thus, then, by the operation of this mobocratic sprit which all must admit is now abroad in the land, the strongest bulwark of any government, and particularly of those constituted like ours, may effectually be broken down and destroyed—I mean the attachment of the people. Whenever this effect shall be produced among us; whenever the vicious portion of population shall be permitted to gather in bands of hundreds and thousands, and burn churches, ravage and rob provision stores, throw printing presses into rivers, shoot editors, and hang and burn obnoxious persons at pleasure and with impunity, depend on it, this government cannot last. By such things the feelings of the best citizens will become more or less alienated from it, and thus it will be left without friends, or with too few, and those few too weak to make their friendship effectual. At such a time, and under such circumstances, men of sufficient talent and ambition will not be wanting to seize the opportunity, strike the blow, and overturn that fair fabric which for the last half century has been the fondest hope of the lovers of freedom throughout the world.

I know the American people are much attached to their government; I know they would suffer much for its sake; I know they would endure evils long and patiently before they would ever think of exchanging it for another—yet, notwithstanding all this, if the laws be continually despised and disregarded, if their rights to be secure in their persons and property are held by no better tenure than the caprice of a mob, the alienation of their affections from the government is the natural consequence; and to that, sooner or later, it must come.

Here, then, is one point at which danger may be expected.

The question recurs, "How shall we fortify against it?" The answer is simple. Let every American, every lover of liberty, every well-wisher to his posterity swear by the blood of the Revolution never to violate in the least particular the laws of the country, and never to tolerate their violation by others. As the patriots of sev-

enty-six did to the support of the Declaration of Independence, so
to the support of the Constitution and laws let every American
pledge his life, his property, and his sacred honor—let every man
remember that to violate the law is to trample on the blood of his
father, and to tear the charter of his own and his children's liberty.
Let reverence for the laws be breathed by every American mother
to the lisping babe that prattles on her lap; let it be taught in
schools, in seminaries, and in colleges; let it be written in primers,
spelling books, and in almanacs; let it be preached from the pulpit,
proclaimed in legislative halls, and enforced in courts of justice.
And, in short, let it become the political religion of the nation;
and let the old and the young, the rich and the poor, the grave and
the gay of all sexes and tongues and colors and conditions, sacrifice unceasingly upon its altars.

While ever a state of feeling such as this shall universally or
even very generally prevail throughout the nation, vain will be
every effort, and fruitless every attempt, to subvert our national
freedom.

When I so pressingly urge a strict observance of all the laws, let
me not be understood as saying there are no bad laws, or that
grievances may not arise for the redress of which no legal provisions have been made. I mean to say no such thing. But I do mean
to say that although bad laws, if they exist, should be repealed as
soon as possible, still, while they continue in force, for the sake of
example they should be religiously observed. So also in unprovided cases. If such arise, let proper legal provisions be made for
them with the least possible delay, but till then let them, it not too
intolerable, be borne with.

There is no grievance that is a fit object of redress by mob law.
In any case that may arise, as, for instance, the promulgation of
abolitionism, one of two positions is necessarily true—that is, the
thing is right within itself, and therefore deserves the protection
of all law and all good citizens, or it is wrong, and therefore proper
to be prohibited by legal enactments; and in neither case is the interposition of mob law either necessary, justifiable, or excusable.

But it may be asked, "Why suppose danger to our political institutions? Have we not preserved them for more than fifty years? And why may we not for fifty times as long?"

We hope there is not sufficient reason. We hope all danger may be overcome; but to conclude that no danger may ever arise would itself be extremely dangerous. There are now, and will hereafter be, many causes, dangerous in their tendency, which have not existed heretofore, and which are not too insignificant to merit attention. That our government should have been maintained in its original form, from its establishment until now, is not much to be wondered at. It had many props to support it through that period, which now are decayed and crumbled away. Through that period it was felt by all to be an undecided experiment; now it is understood to be a successful one. Then, all that sought celebrity and fame and distinction expected to find them in the success of that experiment. Their all was staked upon it; their destiny was inseparably linked with it. Their ambition aspired to display before an admiring world a practical demonstration of the truth of a proposition which had hitherto been considered at best no better than problematical—namely, the capability of a people to govern themselves. If they succeeded they were to be immortalized; their names were to be transferred to counties, and cities, and rivers, and mountains; and to be revered and sung, toasted through all time. If they failed, they were to be called knaves, and fools, and fanatics for a fleeting hour; then to sink and be forgotten. They succeeded. The experiment is successful, and thousands have won their deathless names in making it so. But the game is caught; and I believe it is true that with the catching end the pleasures of the chase. This field of glory is harvested, and the crop is already appropriated. But new reapers will arise, and they too will seek a field. It is to deny what the history of the world tells us is true, to suppose that men of ambition and talents will not continue to spring up amongst us. And when they do, they will as naturally seek the gratification of their ruling passion as others have done before them. The question then is, can that gratification be found in supporting and maintaining an edifice that has been erected by others? Most certainly it cannot. Many great and good men, sufficiently qualified for any task they should undertake, may ever be found whose ambition would aspire to nothing beyond a seat in Congress, a gubernatorial or a president's chair; but such belong not to the family of the lion, or the tribe of the eagle. What! Think you these places would satisfy an Alexander, a Caesar, or a Napoleon? Never! Towering genius disdains a beaten path. It seeks regions hitherto unexplored. It sees no distinction in adding story to story upon the monuments of fame erected to the memory of others. It denies that it is glory enough to serve under any chief. It scorns to tread in the footsteps of any predecessor, however illustrious. It thirsts and burns for distinction; and if possible, it will have it, whether at the expense of emancipating slaves or enslaving freemen. Is it unreasonable, then, to expect that some man possessed of the loftiest genius, coupled with ambition sufficient to push it to its utmost stretch, will at some time spring up among us? And when such a one does, it will require the people to be united with each other, attached to the government and laws, and generally intelligent, to successfully frustrate his designs.

Distinction will be his paramount object, and although he would as willingly, perhaps more so, acquire it by doing good as harm, yet, that opportunity being past, and nothing left to be done in the way of building up, he would set boldly to the task of pulling down.

Here then is a probable case, highly dangerous, and such a one as could not have well existed heretofore.

Another reason which once was, but which, to the same extent, is now no more, has done much in maintaining our institutions thus far. I mean the powerful influence which the interesting scenes of the Revolution had upon the passions of the people as distinguished from their judgment. By this influence, the jealousy, envy, and avarice incident to our nature, and so common to a state of peace, prosperity, and conscious strength, were for the time in a great measure smothered and rendered inactive, while the deep-

rooted principles of hate, and the powerful motive of revenge, instead of being turned against each other, were directed exclusively
against the British nation. And thus, from the force of circumstances, the basest principles of our nature were either made to lie
dormant, or to become the active agents in the advancement of
the noblest of causes—that of establishing and maintaining civil
and religious liberty.

But this state of feeling must fade, is fading, had faded, with the
circumstances that produced it.

I do not mean to say that the scenes of the Revolution are now
or ever will be entirely forgotten, but that, like everything else,
they must fade upon the memory of the world, and grow more
and more dim by the lapse of time. In history, we hope, they will
be read of, and recounted, so long as the Bible shall be read; but
even granting that they will, their influence cannot be what it
heretofore has been. Even then they cannot be so universally
known nor so vividly felt as they were by the generation just gone
to rest. At the close of that struggle, nearly every adult male had
been a participator in some of its scenes. The consequence was
that of those scenes, in the form of a husband, a father, a son, or a
brother, a living history was to be found in every family—a history
bearing the indubitable testimonies of its own authenticity, in the
limbs mangled, in the scars of wounds received, in the midst of
the very scenes related—a history, too, that could be read and understood alike by all, the wise and the ignorant, the learned and
the unlearned. But those histories are gone. They can be read no
more forever. They were a fortress of strength; but what invading
foeman could never do, the silent artillery of times has done—the
leveling of its walls. They are gone. They were a forest of giant
oaks; but the all-resistless hurricane has swept over them, and left
only here and there a lonely trunk, despoiled of its verdure, shorn
of its foliage, unshading and unshaded, to murmur in a few more
gentle breezes, and to combat with its mutilated limbs a few more
ruder storms, then to sink and be no more.

They were the pillars of the temple of liberty; and now that they have crumbled away that temple must fall unless we, their descendants, supply their places with other pillars, hewn from the solid quarry of sober reason. Passion has helped us, but can do so no more. It will in future be our enemy. Reason—cold, calculating, unimpassioned reason—must furnish all the materials for our future support and defense. Let those materials be molded into general intelligence, sound morality, and, in particular, a reverence for the Constitution and laws; and that we improved to the last, that we remained free to the last, that we revered his name to the last, that during his long sleep we permitted no hostile foot to pass over or desecrate his resting place, shall be that which to learn the last trump shall awaken our Washington.

Upon these let the proud fabric of freedom rest, as the rock of its basis; and as truly as has been said of the only greater institution, "the gates of hell shall not prevail against it."

(NH I, 35–50)

Autobiography

December 20, 1859
Lincoln's autobiographical information, published in Republican newspapers.

My dear Sir:

Herewith is a little sketch, as you requested. There is not much of it, for the reason, I suppose, that there is not much of me. If anything be made out of it, I wish it to be modest, and not to go beyond the material. If it were thought necessary to incorporate anything from any of my speeches, I suppose there would be no objection. Of course it must not appear to have been written by myself.

Yours very truly,
A. Lincoln

I was born February 12, 1809, in Hardin County, Kentucky. My parents were both born in Virginia, of undistinguished families—second families, perhaps I should say. My mother, who died in my tenth year, was of a family of the name of Hanks, some of whom now reside in Adams, and others in Macon County, Illinois. My paternal grandfather, Abraham Lincoln, emigrated from Rockingham County, Virginia, to Kentucky about 1781 or 1782, where a year or two later he was killed by the Indians, not in battle, but by stealth, when he was laboring to open a farm in the forest. His ancestors, who were Quakers, went to Virginia from Berks County, Pennsylvania. An effort to identify them with the New England family of the same name ended in nothing more definite than a similarity of Christian names in both families, such as Enoch, Levi, Mordecai, Solomon, Abraham, and the like.

My father, at the death of his father, was but six years of age, and he grew up literally without education. He removed from Kentucky to what is now Spencer County, Indiana, in my eighth year. We reached our new home about the time the state came into the Union. It was a wild region, with many bears and other wild animals still in the woods. There I grew up. There were some schools, so called, but no qualification was ever required of a teacher beyond "readin, writin, and cipherin" to the Rule of Three. If a straggler supposed to understand Latin happened to sojourn in the neighborhood, he was looked upon as a wizard. There was absolutely nothing to excite ambition for education. Of course, when I came of age I did not know much. Still, somehow, I could read, write, and cipher to the rule of three, but that was all. I have not been to school since. The little advance I now have upon this store of education, I have picked up from time to time under the pressure of necessity.

I was raised to farm work, which I continued till I was twenty-two. At twenty-one I came to Illinois, Macon County. Then I got to New Salem, at that time in Sangamon, now in Menard County, where I remained a year as a sort of clerk in a store. Then came the Black Hawk War; and I was elected a captain of volunteers, a success which gave me more pleasure than any I have had since. I went the campaign, was elected, ran for the legislature the same year (1832), and was beaten—the only time I ever have been beaten by the people. The next and three succeeding biennial elections I was elected to the legislature. I was not a candidate afterward. During this legislative period I had studied law, and removed to Springfield to practice it. In 1846 I was once elected to the Lower House of Congress. Was not a candidate for reelection. From 1848 to 1854, both inclusive, practiced law more assiduously than ever before. Always a Whig in politics; and generally on the Whig electoral tickets, making active canvasses. I was losing interest in politics when the repeal of the Missouri Compromise aroused me again. What I have done since then is pretty well known.

If any personal description of me is thought desirable, it may be said that I am, in height, six feet four inches, nearly; lean in flesh, weighing on average one hundred and eighty pounds; dark complexion, with coarse black hair and gray eyes. No other marks or brands recollected.

Yours truly,
A. Lincoln

(NH V, 286–89)

First Inaugural Address

March 4, 1861
Lincoln's first inaugural address, delivered from the east portico of the U.S. Capitol. An earlier draft, more strident than the version Lincoln delivered, was toned down at the recommendation of several associates.

Fellow citizens of the United States: In compliance with a custom as old as the government itself, I appear before you to address you briefly, and to take in your presence the oath prescribed by the Constitution of the United States to be taken by the president "before he enters on the execution of his office."

I do not consider it necessary at present for me to discuss those matters of administration about which there is no special anxiety or excitement.

Apprehension seems to exist among the people of the Southern states that by the accession of a Republican administration their property and their peace and personal security are to be endangered. There has never been any reasonable cause for such apprehension. Indeed, the most ample evidence to the contrary has all the while existed and been open to their inspection. It is found in nearly all the published speeches of him who now addresses you. I do but quote from one of those speeches when I declare that "I have no purpose, directly or indirectly, to interfere with the institution of slavery in the states where it exists. I believe I have no lawful right to do so, and I have no inclination to do so." Those who nominated and elected me did so with full knowledge that I had made this and many similar declarations, and had never recanted them.

And, more than this, they placed in the platform for my acceptance, and as a law to themselves and to me, the clear and emphatic resolution which I now read:

"Resolved, that the maintenance inviolate of the rights of the states, and especially the right of each state to order and control its own domestic institutions according to its own judgment exclusively, is essential to that balance of power on which the perfection and endurance of our political fabric depend, and we denounce the lawless invasion by armed force of the soil of any state or territory, no matter under what pretext, as among the gravest of crimes."

I now reiterate these sentiments; and, in doing so, I only press upon the public attention the most conclusive evidence of which the case is susceptible, that the property, peace, and security of no section are to be in any wise endangered by the now incoming administration. I add, too, that all the protection which, consistently with the Constitution and the laws, can be given, will be cheerfully given to all the states when lawfully demanded, for whatever cause—as cheerfully to one section as to another.

There is much controversy about the delivering up of fugitives from service or labor. The clause I now read is as plainly written in the Constitution as any other of its provisions:

"No person held to service or labor in one state, under the laws thereof, escaping into another, shall in consequence of any law or regulation therein be discharged from such service or labor, but shall be delivered up on the claim of the party to whom such service or labor may be due."

It is scarcely questioned that this provision was intended by those who made it for the reclaiming of what we call fugitive slaves; and the intention of the lawgiver is the law. All members of Congress swear their support to the whole Constitution—to this provision as much as to any other. To the proposition, then, that slaves whose cases come within the terms of this clause "shall be delivered up," their oaths are unanimous. Now, if they would make the effort in good temper, could they not with nearly equal unanimity frame and pass a law by means of which to keep good that unanimous oath?

There is some difference of opinion whether this clause should be enforced by national or by state authority; but surely that difference is not a very material one. If the slave is to be surrendered, it can be of but little consequence to him or to others by which authority it is done. And should anyone in any case be content that his oath shall go unkept on a merely unsubstantial controversy as to how it shall be kept?

Again, in any law upon this subject, ought not all the safeguards of liberty known in civilized and humane jurisprudence to be introduced, so that a free man be not, in any case, surrendered as a slave? And might it not be well at the same time to provide by law for the enforcement of that clause in the Constitution which guarantees that "the citizens of each state shall be entitled to all privileges and immunities of citizens in the several states"?

I take the official oath today with no mental reservations, and with no purpose to construe the Constitution or laws by any hypercritical rules. And while I do not choose now to specify particular acts of Congress as proper to be enforced, I do suggest that it will be much safer for all, both in official and private stations, to conform to and abide by all those acts which stand unrepealed, than to violate any of them, trusting to find impunity in having them held to be unconstitutional.

It is seventy-two years since the first inauguration of a president under our national Constitution. During that period fifteen different and greatly distinguished citizens have, in succession, administered the executive branch of the government. They have conducted it through many perils, and generally with great success. Yet, with all this scope of precedent, I now enter upon the same task for the brief constitutional term of four years under great and peculiar difficulty. A disruption of the Federal Union, heretofore only menaced, is now formidably attempted.

I hold that, in contemplation of universal law and of the Constitution, the Union of these states is perpetual. Perpetuity is implied, if not expressed, in the fundamental law of all national governments. It is safe to assert that no government proper ever had a provision in its organic law for its own termination.

Continue to execute all the express provisions of our National Constitution, and the Union will endure forever—it being impossible to destroy it except by some action not provided for in the instrument itself.

Again, if the United States be not a government proper, but an association of states in the nature of contract merely, can it, as a contract, be peaceably unmade by less than all the parties who made it? One party to a contract may violate it—break it, so to speak; but does it not require all to lawfully rescind it?

Descending from these general principles, we find the proposition that, in legal contemplation the Union is perpetual confirmed by the history of the Union itself. The Union is much older than the Constitution. It was formed, in fact, by the Articles of Association in 1774. It was matured and continued by the Declaration of Independence in 1776. It was further matured, and the faith of all the then thirteen states expressly plighted and engaged that it should be perpetual, by the Articles of Confederation in 1778. And, finally, in 1787 one of the declared objects for ordaining and establishing the Constitution was "to form a more perfect Union."

But if the destruction of the Union by one or by a part only of the states be lawfully possible, the Union is less perfect than before the Constitution, having lost the vital element of perpetuity.

It follows from these views that no state upon its own mere motion can lawfully get out of the Union; that resolves and ordinances to that effect are legally void; and that acts of violence, within any state or states, against the authority of the United States, are insurrectionary or revolutionary, according to circumstances.

I therefore consider that, in view of the Constitution and the laws, the Union is unbroken; and to the extent of my ability I shall take care, as the Constitution itself expressly enjoins upon me, that the laws of the Union be faithfully executed in all the states. Doing this I deem to be only a simple duty on my part; and I shall perform it so far as practicable, unless my rightful masters, the American people, shall withhold the requisite means, or in some authoritative manner direct the contrary. I trust this will not be regarded as a menace, but only as the declared purpose of the Union that it will constitutionally defend and maintain itself.

In doing this there needs to be no bloodshed or violence; and there shall be none, unless it be forced upon the national authority. The power confided to me will be used to hold, occupy, and possess the property and places belonging to the government, and to collect the duties and imposts; but beyond what may be necessary for these objects, there will be no invasion, no using of force against or among the people anywhere. Where hostility to the United States, in any interior locality, shall be so great and universal as to prevent competent resident citizens from holding the federal offices, there will be no attempt to force obnoxious strangers among the people for that object. While the strict legal right may exist in the government to enforce the exercise of these offices, the attempt to do so would be so irritating, and so nearly impracticable withal, that I deem it better to forego for the time the uses of such offices.

The mails, unless repelled, will continue to be furnished in all parts of the Union. So far as possible, the people everywhere shall have that sense of perfect security which is most favorable to calm thought and reflection. The course here indicated will be followed unless current events and experience shall show a modification or change to be proper, and in every case and exigency my best discretion will be exercised according to circumstances actually existing, and with a view and a hope of a peaceful solution of the national troubles and the restoration of fraternal sympathies and affections.

That there are persons in one section or another who seek to destroy the Union at all events, and are glad of any pretext to do it, I will neither affirm nor deny; but if there be such, I need address no word to them. To those, however, who really love the Union, may I not speak?

Before entering upon so grave a matter as the destruction of our national fabric, with all its benefits, its memories, and its hopes, would it not be wise to ascertain precisely why we do it? Will you hazard so desperate a step while there is any possibility that any portion of the ills you fly from have no real existence? Will you, while the certain ills you fly to are greater than all the real ones you fly from—will you risk the commission of so fearful a mistake?

All profess to be content in the Union if all constitutional rights can be maintained. Is it true, then, that any right, plainly written in the Constitution, has been denied? I think not. Happily the human mind is so constituted that no party can reach to the audacity of doing this. Think, if you can, of a single instance in which a plainly written provision of the Constitution has ever been denied. If by the mere force of numbers a majority should deprive a minority of any clearly written constitutional right, it might, in a moral point of view, justify revolution—certainly would if such a right were a vital one. But such is not our case. All the vital rights of minorities and of individuals are so plainly assured to them by affirmations and negations, guarantees and prohibitions, in the Constitution, that controversies never arise concerning them. But no organic law can ever be framed with a provision specifically applicable to every question which may occur in practical administration. No foresight can anticipate, nor any document of reasonable length contain, express provisions for all possible questions. Shall fugitives from labor be surrendered by national or by state authority? The Constitution does not expressly say. *May* Congress prohibit slavery in the Territories? The Constitution does not expressly say. *Must* Congress protect slavery in the Territories? The Constitution does not expressly say.

From questions of this class spring all our constitutional controversies, and we divide upon them into majorities and minorities. If the minority will not acquiesce, the majority must, or the government must cease. There is no other alternative; for continuing the government is acquiescence on one side or the other.

If a minority in such case will secede rather than acquiesce, they make a precedent which in turn will divide and ruin them; for a minority of their own will secede from them whenever a majority refuses to be controlled by such minority. For instance, why may not any portion of a new confederacy a year or two hence arbitrarily secede again, precisely as portions of the present Union now claim to secede from it? All who cherish disunion sentiments are now being educated to the exact temper of doing this.

Is there such perfect identity of interests among the states to compose a new Union, as to produce harmony only, and prevent renewed secession?

Plainly, the central idea of secession is the essence of anarchy. A majority held in restraint by constitutional checks and limitations, and always changing easily with deliberate changes of popular opinions and sentiments, is the only true sovereign of a free people. Whoever rejects it does, of necessity, fly to anarchy or to despotism. Unanimity is impossible; the rule of a minority, as a permanent arrangement, is wholly inadmissible; so that, rejecting the majority principle, anarchy or despotism in some form is all that is left.

I do not forget the position, assumed by some, that constitutional questions are to be decided by the Supreme Court; nor do I deny that such decisions must be binding, in any case, upon the parties to a suit, as to the object of that suit, while they are also entitled to very high respect and consideration in all parallel cases by all other departments of the government. And while it is obviously possible that such decision may be erroneous in any given case, still the evil effect following it, being limited to that particular case, with the chance that it may be overruled and never become a precedent for other cases, can better be borne than could the evils of a different practice.

At the same time, the candid citizen must confess that if the policy of the government, upon vital questions affecting the whole people, is to be irrevocably fixed by decisions of the Supreme Court, the instant they are made, in ordinary litigation between parties in personal actions, the people will have ceased to be their own rulers, having to that extent practically resigned their government into the hands of that eminent tribunal. Nor is there in this view any assault upon the court or the judges. It is a duty from which they may not shrink to decide cases properly brought before them, and it is no fault of theirs if others seek to turn their decisions to political purposes.

One section of our country believes slavery is right, and ought to be extended, while the other believes it is wrong, and ought not to be extended. This is the only substantial dispute. The fugitive slave clause of the Constitution, and the law for the suppression of the foreign slave trade, are each as well enforced, perhaps, as any law can ever be in a community where the moral sense of the people imperfectly supports the law itself. The great body of the people abide by the dry legal obligation in both cases, and a few break over in each. This, I think, cannot be perfectly cured; and it would be worse in both cases after the separation of the sections than before. The foreign slave trade, now imperfectly suppressed, would be ultimately revived, without restriction, in one section, while fugitive slaves, now only partially surrendered, would not be surrendered at all by the other.

Physically speaking, we cannot separate. We cannot remove our respective sections from each other, nor build an impassable wall between them. A husband and wife may be divorced, and go out of the presence and beyond the reach of each other; but the different parts of our country cannot do this. They cannot but remain face to face, and intercourse, either amicable or hostile, must continue between them. Is it possible, then, to make that intercourse more advantageous or more satisfactory after separation than before? Can aliens make treaties easier than friends can make laws? Suppose you go to war, you cannot fight always; and when, after much loss on both sides, and no gain either, you cease fighting, the identical old questions as to terms of intercourse are again upon you.

This country, with its institutions, belongs to the people who inhabit it. Whenever they shall grow weary of the existing government, they can exercise their constitutional right of amending it, or their revolutionary right to dismember or overthrow it. I cannot be ignorant of the fact that many worthy and patriotic citizens are desirous of having the National Constitution amended. While I make no recommendation of amendments, I fully recognize the rightful authority of the people over the whole subject, to be exercised in either of the modes prescribed in the instrument itself; and I should, under existing circumstances, favor rather than oppose a fair opportunity being afforded the people to act upon it. I will venture to add that to me the convention mode seems preferable, in that it allows amendments to originate with the people themselves, instead of only permitting them to take or reject propositions originated by others not specially chosen for that purpose, and which might not be precisely such as they would wish to either accept or refuse. I understand a proposed amendment to the Constitution—which amendment, however, I have not seen—has passed Congress, to the effect that the federal government shall never interfere with the domestic institutions of the states, including that of persons held to service. To avoid misconstruction of what I have said, I depart from my purpose not to speak of particular amendments so far as to say that, holding such a provision to not be implied constitutional law, I have no objection to its being made express and irrevocable.

The chief magistrate derives all his authority from the people, and they have conferred none upon him to fix terms for the separation of the states. The people themselves can do this also if they choose; but the executive, as such, has nothing to do with it. His duty is to administer the present government, as it came to his hands, and to transmit it, unimpaired by him, to his successor.

Why should there not be a patient confidence in the ultimate justice of the people? Is there any better or equal hope in the world? In our present differences is either party without faith of being in the right? If the Almighty Ruler of Nations, with is eternal truth and justice, be on your side of the North, or on yours of the South, that truth and that justice will surely prevail by the judgment of this great tribunal of the American people.

By the frame of the government under which we live, this same people have wisely given their public servants but little power for mischief; and have, with equal wisdom provided for the return of that little to their own hands at very short intervals. While the people retain their virtue and vigilance, no administration, by any extreme of wickedness or folly, can very seriously injure the government in the short space of four years.

My countrymen, one and all, think calmly and well upon this whole subject. Nothing valuable can be lost by taking time. If there be an object to hurry any of you in hot haste to a step which you would never take deliberately, that object will be frustrated by taking time; but no good object can be frustrated by it. Such of you as are now dissatisfied, still have the old Constitution unimpaired, and, on the sensitive point, the laws of your own framing under it; while the new administration will have no immediate power, if it would, to change either. If it were admitted that you who are dissatisfied hold the right side of the dispute, there still is no single good reason for precipitate action. Intelligence, patriotism, Christianity, and a firm reliance on him who has never yet forsaken this favored land, are still competent to adjust in the best way all our present difficulty.

In your hands, my dissatisfied fellow countrymen, and not in mine, is the momentous issue of civil war. The government will not assail you. You can have no conflict without being yourselves the aggressors. You have no oath registered in heaven to destroy the government, while I shall have the most solemn one to "preserve, protect, and defend it."

I am loath to close. We are not enemies, but friends. We must not be enemies. Though passion may have strained, it must not break our bonds of affection. The mystic chords of memory, stretching from every battlefield and patriot grave to every living heart and hearthstone all over this broad land, will yet swell the chorus of the Union when again touched, as surely they will be, by the better angels of our nature.

(NH VI, 169–85)

Appendix D

Condolence Letter to Ephraim and Phoebe Ellsworth

May 25, 1861
A letter written to console the parents of Colonel Elmer E.
Ellsworth, who was killed during the capture of Alexandria,
Virginia. Ellsworth was a friend who had served in Lincoln's
law office.

My Dear Sir and Madam:

In the untimely loss of your noble son, our affliction here is
scarcely less than your own. So much of promised usefulness to
one's country, and of bright hopes for one's self and friends, have
rarely been so suddenly dashed as in his fall. In size, in years, and
in youthful appearance a boy only, his power to command men
was surpassingly great. This power, combined with a fine intellect,
an indomitable energy, and a taste altogether military, constituted
in him, as seemed to me, the best natural talent in that department I ever knew.

And yet he was singularly modest and deferential in social intercourse. My acquaintance with him began less than two years
ago; yet through the latter half of the intervening period it was as
intimate as the disparity of our ages and my engrossing engage-
ments would permit. To me he appeared to have no indulgences
or pastimes; and I never heard him utter a profane or an intem-
perate word. What was conclusive of his good heart, he never forgot his parents. The honors he labored for so laudable, and for which
in the sad end he so gallantly gave his life, he meant for them no
less than for himself.

In the hope that it may be no intrusion upon the sacredness of your sorrow, I have ventured to address you this tribute to the memory of my young friend and your brave and early fallen child.

May God give you that consolation which is beyond all earthly power. Sincerely your friend in a common affliction,

A. Lincoln

(CW IV, 385–86)

Gettysburg Address

November 19, 1863
President Lincoln's immortal two-minute dedication at the Gettysburg National Cemetery.

Fourscore and seven years ago our fathers brought forth on this continent a new nation, conceived in liberty, and dedicated to the proposition that all men are created equal.

Now we are engaged in a great civil war, testing whether that nation, or any nation so conceived and so dedicated, can long endure. We are met on a great battlefield of that war. We have come to dedicate a portion of that field as a final resting-place for those who here gave their lives that that nation might live. It is altogether fitting and proper that we should do this.

But, in a larger sense, we cannot dedicate—we cannot consecrate—we cannot hallow—this ground. The brave men, living and dead, who struggled here, have consecrated it far above our poor power to add or detract. The world will little note nor long remember what we say here, but it can never forget what they did here. It is for us, the living, rather, to be dedicated here to the unfinished work which they who fought here have thus far so nobly advanced. It is rather for us to be here dedicated to the great task remaining before us—that from these honored dead we take increased devotion to that cause for which they gave the last full measure of devotion; that we here highly resolve that these dead shall not have died in vain; that this nation, under God, shall have a new birth of freedom; and that government of the people, by the people, for the people, shall not perish from the earth.

(NH IX, 209–10)

Appendix F

Condolence Letter to Lydia Bixby

November 21, 1864
Letter of condolence to Lydia Bixby of Boston, whose five sons were killed in the Civil War.

Dear Madam:

I have been shown in the files of the War Department a statement of the Adjutant-General of Massachusetts that you are the mother of five sons who have died gloriously on the field of battle. I feel how weak and fruitless must be any words of mine which should attempt to beguile you from the grief of a loss so overwhelming. But I cannot refrain from tendering to you the consolation that may be found in the thanks of the Republic they died to save. I pray that our heavenly Father may assuage the anguish of your bereavement, and leave you only the cherished memory of the loved and lost, and the solemn pride that must be yours to have laid so costly a sacrifice upon the altar of freedom.

(NH X, 274–75)

Second Inaugural Address

March 4, 1865
Lincoln's second inaugural address, which, though initially not
well received by the press, was later recognized as one of his great-
est speeches.

Fellow countrymen: At this second appearing to take the oath of
the presidential office, there is less occasion for an extended address than there was at the first. Then a statement, somewhat in
detail, of a course to be pursued, seemed fitting and proper. Now,
at the expiration of four years, during which public declarations
have been constantly called forth on every point and phase of the
great contest which still absorbs the attention and engrosses the
energies of the nation, little that is new could be presented. The
progress of our arms, upon which all else chiefly depends, is as well
known to the public as myself; and it is, I trust, reasonably satisfactory and encouraging to all. With high hope for the future, no
prediction in regard to it is ventured.

On the occasion corresponding to this four years ago, all
thoughts were anxiously directed to an impending civil war. All
dreaded it—all sought to avert it. While the inaugural address was
being delivered from this place, devoted altogether to saving the
Union without war, insurgent agents were in the city seeking to
destroy it without war—seeking to dissolve the Union, and divide
effects, by negotiation. Both parties deprecated war; but one of
them would make war rather than let the nation survive; and the
other would accept war rather than let it perish. And the war
came.

One-eighth of the whole population were colored slaves, not

distributed generally over the Union, but localized in the Southern part of it. These slaves constituted a peculiar and powerful interest. All knew that this interest was, somehow, the cause of the war. To strengthen, perpetuate, and extend this interest was the object for which the insurgents would rend the Union, even by war; while the government claimed no right to do more than to restrict the territorial enlargement of it.

Neither party expected for the war the magnitude or the duration which it has already attained. Neither anticipated that the cause of the conflict might cease with, or even before, the conflict itself should cease. Each looked for an easier triumph, and a result fundamental and astounding. Both read the same Bible, and pray to the same God; and each invokes his aid against the other. It may seem strange that any men should dare to ask a just God's assistance in wringing their bread from the sweat of other men's faces; but let us judge not, that we be not judged. The prayers of both could not be answered—that of neither has been answered fully.

The Almighty has his own purposes. "Woe unto the world because of offenses! For it must needs be that offenses come; but woe to that man by whom the offense cometh." If we shall suppose that American slavery is one of those offenses which, in the providence of God, must needs come, but which, having continued through his appointed time, he now wills to remove, and that he gives to both North and South this terrible war, as the woe due to those by whom the offense came, shall we discern therein any departure from those divine attributes which the believers in a living God always ascribe to him? Fondly we hope—fervently do we pray—that this mighty scourge of war may speedily pass away. Yet, if God wills that it continue until all the wealth piled by the bondsman's two hundred and fifty years of unrequited toil shall be sunk, and until every drop of blood drawn with the lash shall be paid by another drawn with the sword, as was said three thousand years ago, so still it must be said, "The judgments of the Lord are true and righteous altogether."

With malice toward none; with charity for all; with firmness in the right, as God gives us to see the right, let us strive on to finish the work we are in; to bind up the nation's wounds; to care for him who shall have borne the battle, and for his widow, and his orphan—to do all which may achieve and cherish a just and lasting peace among ourselves, and with all nations.

(NH XI, 45–47)

Sources

KEY TO TEXT SOURCES

CW   The Collected Works of Abraham Lincoln. 10 vols.
NH   Complete Works of Abraham Lincoln. 8 vols.

SELECTED BIBLIOGRAPHY

Basler, Roy P., ed. *The Collected Works of Abraham Lincoln.* New Brunswick, N.J.: Rutgers University Press, 1953.

Donald, David Herbert. *Lincoln.* New York: Simon & Schuster, 1995.

Miers, Earl Schenk, ed. *Lincoln Day by Day: A Chronology.* Washington, D.C.: Lincoln Sesquicentennial Commission, 1960.

Miller, William Lee. *Lincoln's Virtues: An Ethical Biography.* New York: Random House, 2002.

Neely, Mark E. *The Last Best Hope of Earth: Abraham Lincoln and the Promise of America.* Cambridge, Mass.: Harvard University Press, 1993.

Nicholas, John G. and John Hay, eds. *Complete Works of Abraham Lincoln.* Harrogate, Tenn.: Lincoln Memorial University, 1894.

Oates, Stephen B. *With Malice Toward None: The Life of Abraham Lincoln.* New York: Harper & Row, 1977.

Peterson, Merrill D. *Lincoln in American Memory.* New York: Oxford University Press, 1994.

Wilson, Douglas L. *Honor's Voice: The Transformation of Abraham Lincoln.* New York: Random House, 1998.

Online Resources

Abraham Lincoln Papers, Library of Congress
memory.loc.gov/ammem/alhtml/malhome.html

Abraham Lincoln Presidential Library & Museum
alincoln-library.com

Lincoln Home, National Park Service
www.nps.gov/liho

Lincoln/Net, Northern Illinois University
lincoln.lib.niu.edu

Mr. Lincoln's Virtual Library, Library of Congress
memory.loc.gov/ammem/alhtml/alhome.html

Mr. Lincoln's White House, The Lehrman Institute
www.mrlincolnswhitehouse.org/index.html